My Challenge to Financial Engineering at the age of 44

Jongnam Kim

Contents

Preface 1

Part 1. First Semester (Fall 2017) 3

1.1 School: First Semester is the Hardest 5

1.2 English: Missing Half of Listening 26

1.3 Life: Car-Centric Country 31

1.4 Parenting: Kids Increase Entropy 54

1.5 Culture: People are All Alike 68

Part 2. Second Semester (Spring 2018) 75

2.1 School: Class Notes with Touch-Pen 77

2.2 English: Speaking to Oneself 100

2.3 Life: Where is Spring? 104

2.4 Parenting: Co-Parenting with YouTube 116

2.5 Culture: Volunteer Society 125

Part 3. Summer Break (Summer 2018) 129

3.1 U.S. West Car Trip 131

3.2 Travel to Illinois 188

3.3 Summer Life 220

Part 4. Last Semester (Fall 2018) 239

4.1 School: Future of Financial Engineering 240

4.2 English: Read English Books Aloud 255

4.3 Life: Don't Ask a Human 263

4.4 Parenting: Infantile Dependency Needs 277

4.5 Culture: Remember Through Donation 288

Closing 293

Preface

I planned two books in a series, and this book is the first one of them. The title of this book is "My Challenge to Financial Engineering at the age of 44" and the second one (aim to publish in this winter) is "My Coursework in Financial Engineering at the age of 44."

The reasons why I wrote these books are as follows.

First, I needed to record and organize what I studied at the graduate school for myself because it is a human memory that fades over time unless written down. And contents only become my own when I can reconstruct them through my expression. I tried to write the stories in detail so that they could be useful for those who are interested in studying financial engineering or studying abroad.

Secondly, I wanted to make meaningful results as I was studying abroad at a high cost. I planned to study abroad for my company's overseas education program and receive financial support for tuition and living expenses. But, the issue of exceeding the initially announced one-year period by about four months eventually forced me to come at my own cost through a leave of absence. Not only monetary damages, but also my relationship with the company suffered a lot, and above all, I realized I am not an influential person in my society. I wrote this book in a way that made me look back and re-establish myself in the far-off U.S. from Korea.

Lastly, I wanted to leave my efforts as a father to my children. I wanted to show that I had a challenging life with courage, even though I was afraid of uncertainty in life. My daughter, Taeju and my son, Taye are still busy in fighting for more snacks today, but if they read this book later, they will know that dad loved Taeju and Taye much and tried to live a beautiful life with his families.

Most of all, I wanted to write such a book, not a book that people read once and neglect it, but a book that is taken out and read whenever they need it.

In the summer of 2019 at Urbana-Champaign

Jongnam Kim

Marcus Aurelius' <Meditations> book, which was quoted in the middle of this book, refers to Penguin Classics, 2006.

Part 1. First Semester (Fall 2017)

It is my first semester in the United States. To begin with, I got unsatisfactory results in both English and academic performance. I failed to take the initiative in both English speaking and financial engineering study. I was barely able to survive. And our family's adaptation to the U.S. is also no more than survival.

I am not used to my homework or exams since I came back to school from work for more than ten years. It is not easy to get good grades even though I study until midnight. There are a lot of students who do well on the test, and I feel like I am average at best in my majors.

Also, I hardly invested in studying English. Though the coursework was conducted in English and exposed to English more than in Korea, our class was mostly Chinese, so we did not use English not much. When I go to church or Bible study, I used English, but I do not feel that English training is possible with a short and limited conversation. No one is trying to correct my wrong English directly and it is a conversation in broken English with most international students. And because they are not confident, they tend to babble, making it harder to understand. Instead, it is easier to understand conversations with people who are good at English, including Americans, but the problem is that Americans do not take much time to me.

The school was fun in its way, and I liked learning financial engineering, which is a convergence study. For programming tasks in C ++, it was interesting to implement option pricing directly in a variety of ways and understand the principles. The economics professor's approach was better than studying in Korea, and the class that combines newspaper article reading was refreshing.

However, all the subjects had too much homework, so it was hard to prepare for class or study for exams. Because problem set comes out on a biweekly basis and programming homework is available every week, I have never rested doing my homework on weekends. The problem was also tricky, so it took at least two days to find an answer, and even that was often incorrect.

My wife played many roles at home. First of all, she enjoys living in the U.S. and studying English. But it's always hard for her to take care of children alone, so I try to find my role as a father and have children with me. It also seems a little uneasy that my wife is taking a leave of absence from work due to paternity leave.

Taeju is a full five-year-old girl who is doing well in the U.S. and enjoys watching English videos. But her English speaking is rudimentary yet, so she feels stressed and frustrated when she plays with her friends at school.

Taye is two years old now since he came to America and seems to be slow of speech. He can't say anything other than simple words such as mom and dad. However, He likes here more because he spends more time with his mom. He rarely catches a cold than when he was in Korea. If he loses the battle with his older sister to take over his mom, he cries out very loudly.

1.1 School: First Semester is the Hardest

University of Illinois & Financial Engineering

The University of Illinois at Urbana-Champaign is a state university located across two cities, Urbana and Champaign, Illinois. It is usually called 'UIUC' or 'U of I.' It was founded in 1867, so it is now 150 years old. The University of Illinois system itself has three campuses in Chicago, Springfield, and Urbana-Champaign. UIUC is the main campus.

The U.S. was facing a period of rapid industrialization after the Civil War (1861-1865), and the state of Illinois established the Illinois Industrial University in Urbana and renamed as the University of Illinois in 1885. Since World War II (1939-1945), it has grown rapidly with a significant increase in the number of students and increased state support, and since 1982, it began attaching its local name 'Urbana-Campaign' behind it to distinguish it from the branch campus in Springfield and Chicago.

UIUC Main Quadrangle

About 200,000 people live in the twin cities of Urbana and Champaign. Urbana is a quiet, typical townhouse with its east side of the school, and Champaign is in the west and feels like an emerging development area with considerable commercial facilities. In a nearby metropolis, it is located in the middle of a triangle in Chicago, Indianapolis and St. Louis, all three of which are two to three hours' drive from here.

I live in a graduate family housing located to the south of the school, the Orchard Downs in Urbana. Here is a university city, so the schedule of the residents' lives depends on the plan of the university's academic affairs. During the vacation, the bus runs diminish, and church service hours are adjusted.

The total number of students at UIUC is about 45,000, of which international students are about 25 percent with about 12,000. Engineering schools are especially well-known for their reputations, and management and accounting are also renowned for their excellent programs. MS in Financial Engineering, which I am attending, is a three-semester program aimed at 'quant' job of financial companies. It is a cooperative program between the engineering school and the business school. The current class size is about 65 people per year, and the average age is about 24. Its nationality is about 90 percent of that of China, and other countries include India, the United States, Europe, Africa, and South Korea.

Many of the famous alumni also graduated from engineering schools: Marc Andreessen, who created the first Web browser Mosaic and Netscape, Max Levchin, co-founder of U.S. electronic payment service PayPal, Nick Holonyak, who first made LEDs in 1965, Jack Welch, former GE chairman, and YouTube founder Steve Chen and Jawed Karim.

Alma mater is a term referring to the university from which one graduated. It means that she is a nourishing mother in Latin. Universities should be like mothers who give students intellectual nourishment to live in society. A statue of Alma mater stands in front of Green Street in the school.

Alma mater statue at the University of Illinois

According to the Wikipedia of Playboy founder Hugh Hefner, his Alma mater is the University of Illinois. Hugh Hefner passed away this year, and the school seems to have rarely promoted that he is from the University of Illinois. When I first looked at Playboy's website more than 20 years ago, I thought that the U.S. made a magazine so starkly, but now, Google search alone has a lot of dirty pictures and videos that make Playboy a decent adult magazine.

Quad Day

Quad is a grass square in the center of the school, and Quad day is a kind of club promotion event held there in August just before the beginning of the fall semester. In August, Illinois, the sun was so hot that if we didn't stay in the shade, our heads would be ripe. But the humidity is not high, so it is cool when you enter the shadow.

It was supposed to be a useful event, but it was not easy for a stroller to go there because there were so many people. Most of all, clubs didn't seem to have any intention of drawing an old-timer like me into their club. They seem to think that the locals pulled a baby stroller to look around. As I took the photo at the end of the event, you can see a lot of free space, but there were huge people in the main quad this day.

Club promotion event at Quad Day

Another event before the start of a semester is 'YMCA Dump and Run.' It is a kind of used donation market, and it is an event where items donated after graduation are displayed at the pavilion, a school grain warehouse, and sold before the fall semester. International students are admitted free of charge. We bought some too, and I think we can get a good deal if we go early.

Donation & used item market (YMCA Dump & Run)

Greek life in the college

The United States had a unique culture called Greek life. A few steps away from the center of the school are many buildings with Greek capital letters such as Alpha, Beta, and Gamma, which are their hideout and their history of college life. I have seen some resumes of Chinese students who graduated from a university in the United States saying that they were a member of some Greek.

Sigma Nu, one of the Greek Fraternity

The Greek life categorized into groups of boys called Fraternity and girls called Sorority. The origin is the 'Pi Beta Kappa' of William Mary University in the United States in 1775 and was a group of social interaction and academic discussions. Currently, nature has changed a little, so students are looking for past exam data. After graduation, I think it has strong characteristics of the social network for employment. Anyway, there were rumors of having a sex party and so on, so there are often debates on whether to continue to exist.

On weekends, I've seen dozens of young women get dressed up and leave the building in groups, and it turns out they were all Greeks. According to a website called 'Greek Rank,' UIUC has 48 Fraternities and 33 Sororities now.

College life in the United States seems very lonely. It may be because individualism culture is influential, and there is no drinking culture like Korea. In an article on Greek, an American girl student wrote: I was going to live with my roommate in the school dormitory and eat together, but I was very lonely because my roommate played with her friends. But the point is that I was able to enter Greeks and have a great college life with good people.

There are many international students at school in order of China, India, and Korea, and they make their style of effort. In the process, there is a natural tendency to get together among the same nationality. It is not easy to make small talk in English, so people from the same country naturally gather together. And Indian style English is not easy for foreigners to understand. Some Chinese students graduated from undergraduate schools in the U.S. did not come together in groups like international students but attended in private.

I tried to get along well, regardless of the group. Mainly, I decided to memorize the other person's name and call it. It is never easy to pronounce and remember names of Chinese and Indian students.

The first semester is the hardest

I spent my first semester in the U.S. graduate school. Sometimes I regret why I am willing to go through this suffering.

First, it is challenging to take a class, take a test, have a quiz, and compete with classmates who are 20 years younger than me. Everyone has their confidence in their studies, and the average point is very high on tests and quiz. Chinese or Indian students seem to be used to this competition from an early age, and some of them seem to be talented. On the other hand, some often did cheat on homework or exams.

Grainger Engineering Library

Second, the American style attitude, such as asking and visiting the professor and talking about small things, was not familiar. The human world is not perfect, so the reality is that living a modest life doesn't give what I want. Furthermore, American universities are actively demanding that students develop relationships with professors, teaching assistants, and fellow students. International students have a lack of this attitude compared to American students. I felt the professors didn't mind students asking such a small question in class. Students who were comfortable with English led the questioning, and I was in a hurry to understand their sayings.

Third, I did not have much time to discuss with my classmates about the class, assignment, or test questions. They often answer roughly, and in fact, most students can do well on tests, but they don't even know enough to explain to others. Next semester, I will have to utilize more professors and develop my English and financial engineering skills so that I can make conversations more actively. It's already started, and it's not easy to get here, so I'd better be more confident on my own.

Don't be depressed or frustrated. Marcus Aurelius also says so in the <Meditations> book. (Book5, 9)

"If you have taken a fall, come back again, and be glad if most of your actions are on the right side of humanity. And love what you return to."

Academic writing class

The required score of TOEFL iBT for the University of Illinois was 103 points, and the average of the MSFE class was about 105 out of 120 points.

I didn't meet the score of 103, so I was given a separate English writing class after taking the university's assessment before the semester. Many international students should take such a required English class. However, as my curriculum was very tight, I felt burdened by this English class and assignments.

It required homework every weekend, and even I wrote a research paper on my major in this English writing class. As a result, I feel proud to have a writing sample, and I was lucky to meet a good teacher named Qinchun (Sunny) Li. Anyway, it was a must for me, and if I am going to take it, I think it is best to make it in the first semester.

Academic writing class photo

Office hours

The office hours are about one or two hours a week for each subject, and it is an official time for students to visit and ask questions and counseling to the professor. If it is not this time, students have to set up an appointment with the professor separately, but it is not plausible due to the professor's busy schedule. Some professors notified office hours by e-mail, not weekly, but once or twice a month.

I used office hours twice this semester. Today, I have been to the office hours of the subject of Economics for the first time. During the office hours, it was hard to talk to the professor one-on-one, because there were already several students who were talking to her, and I barely spoke to her and only got my midterm exam back. I think that students who graduate from the U.S. or are good at English are more actively participating, and international students who are the first semester of U.S. studies, like me, feel uncomfortable.

Library carrel

Carrel's definition shows on Google: a small cubicle with a desk for the use of a reader or student in a library. In some parts of the library, there are separate desks for reading or studying. Two years ago, I went to the University of Hawaii at Hilo, Big Island, and it looked so good because there were so many individual desks in the library that students could study quietly.

The University of Illinois has too many students to spare desks, but there are still quite a few carrels in the library. Carrel from the main library is a separate room in the library. I have to apply to the library for each semester and get

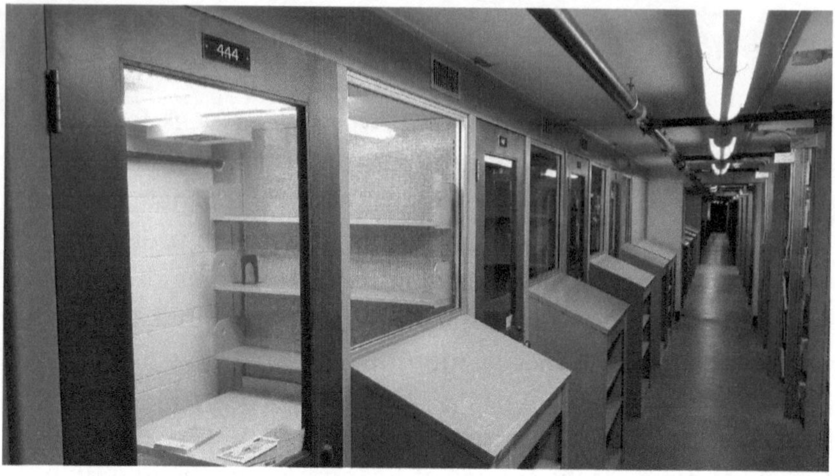

Carrel in the Main Library

my keys, but I felt so stuffy that I went there for the first time and didn't go anymore.

On the other hand, the carols in the engineering library are more open space, so it's good to study, but since the person who put the bag here is the owner, it's not easy to get a seat during the semester, and there are many students passing by looking for an empty carrel, so it's very distracting.

Eating lunch

After coming to the U.S., I sometimes miss the restaurant in the basement of SK V1, Knowledge Industry Center in front of my house in Korea. It's heaven to be able to have that level of lunch and dinner for $5. It's hard to imagine in America.

U.S. universities don't have restaurants like student restaurants in Korea. There are several restaurants in the basement of the Illini Union, the equivalent of a student center, but there seems to be little to eat except hamburgers and snacks. I'm not a picky eater, but I don't have anything to eat. And it's expensive even though there's nothing special.

The Subway burger is cheap and huge, but it is cold. I usually go to Jimmy John's Burger or McDonald's, though sometimes eat in Korean restaurants or Chinese restaurants. These days, I bring boiled eggs, chocolate bars, and coffee, and I have a quick meal in the library reading a newspaper. It is enough for lunch because I have a full breakfast and dinner at home.

Illini Union building

There are also many students who eat in the library after packing in a food truck outside. What surprised me is that they packed the smelly food and ate it in the library carrels without considering others. Sometimes an employee of the library comes up to ask to refrain it when another student reports to the library office.

There are some things to eat around Green Street, where shops are located, including Korean restaurants. After arriving in the United States, my family had McMorning in Green Street McDonald by bus. Anyway, in the U.S., it is better to buy ingredients at a supermarket and cook at home instead of eating out. It's better in terms of price, taste, and distance.

Restroom in the United States

Public restrooms here clearly reveal whether there are people in the toilet because the lower and upper parts are open, and the door is covering only the torso and face. My classmate who immigrated to Chicago in high school once said he was suspended a day from school. The reason is that when he was using the restroom of his school, another student crawled down under the bottom so hit him in anger.

Men's restroom in the Engineering Library

There isn't even any rack to hang bags or clothes, so I see everyone putting their bags on the floor when they use a toilet. Perhaps due to the nature of the United States, it seems trying to prevent problems such as taking drugs or committing suicide in the bathroom. Strangely, the bathroom floor here is relatively clean. I don't think a cleaning guy comes in and takes care of it, either. I've never met a cleaning guy during the day.

Bathrooms at home are also kept dry, with no water outside the bathtub. At first, it was very uncomfortable, but it also has the advantage of not getting damp in the bathroom and not being afraid to slip off the floor. Also, the structure without the threshold of a room can be suitable for kids and the elderly.

McKinley Health Center

During summer, I sweat a lot, and because of long distance flights, I got a relapse of my toe eczema. Notably, unlike in my company, I always wear gym shoes in school, so I sweat a lot. I was treated for toe eczema at McKinley Health Center before I began my semester.

School tuition already includes the fee for using the McKinley Center. There were usually many older doctors, but they seem to be comfortable and reasonable in their way. After the nurse makes necessary inquiries, I finally get to see a doctor, which makes it difficult to tell the difference between a doctor and a nurse because there are many male nurses here. The examination concluded that it was eczema caused by fungi, and said it was essential to dry the feet. When I knew the exact cause, I felt comfortable, and I could recover quickly with the prescribed ointment.

During the school year, I suffered greatly from pain in my left shoulder. Three months ago, while crossing a monkey bar at the playground with one hand, I felt a sharp pain in my left shoulder. I thought about the sentence to speak to the doctor

School hospital, McKinley Health Center

and went. "I hurt my left arm crossing the monkey bar in the playground with one hand." As anyone who has tried it knows, the conversations they give and take while explaining their symptoms at the hospital are much more complicated than in everyday English.

I went to McKinley Hospital during the winter vacation, and my doctor thought there was no major problem with X-rays, and she asked me to take physical therapy at the Center. I thought there might be something wrong with the tendon or ligaments, and I was worried about the MRI cost, but it was a completely different prescription. Anyway, explaining the cause and symptoms of the injury was not as easy as the last toe eczema.

A physical therapist prescribed five exercises at home because they don't seem to have torn apart, and their blood seems to have clumps. Two of the exercise prescriptions are for using T-band, so I received a yellow band. Every time I went there, I got some new exercises, and the intensity of the band was different by color, so my house was full of yellow, red, and blue bands.

Most schools have these health centers, and students will already have their fee included in tuition. The University of Illinois offers essential medical treatment for internal medicine and surgeons, and regular medications such as cold medicine and Tylenol are always available.

T-band exercise prescription

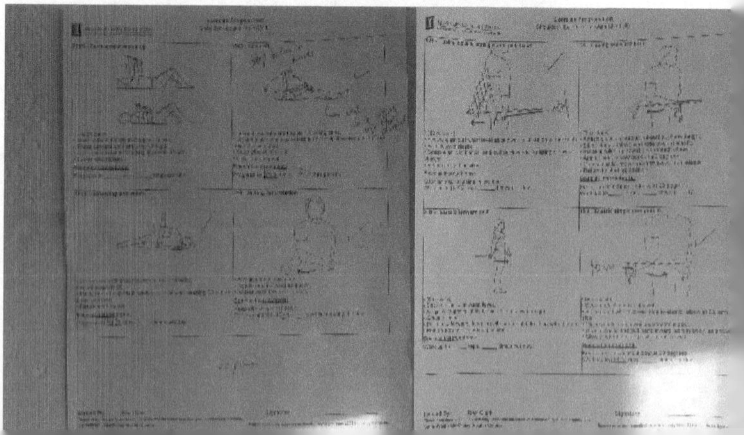

Gies College of Business

I went to the Gies Business School event. Just like the Booth Business School at the University of Chicago, all the prestigious business schools have the name after big donors, and this time, the University of Illinois was also named.

Gies Business School ceremony

Mr. Gies (as pronounced by the goose's plural 'geese') is a Chicago businessman who graduated from the University of Illinois accounting, and this time the alumni couple donated 150 million dollars together, the largest donation in school history and an unusually large amount for the United States as a whole. In terms of Korean won, it is worth 170 billion won.

One of my life's goals is to make 100 billion won, and I'm already frustrated that he donated 170 billion won. As in the picture, we took Mr. Gies to the business school building and held an event. The master's program in financial engineering spanned both business school and engineering school, so I was also present.

Chicago field trip (Nov.16-17, 2017)

I went on a group bus for two days for a Chicago field trip. It was time to visit major financial companies such as the Federal Reserve Bank of Chicago, CTC, CME, and CBOE, and to listen to explanations and ask questions. I was impressed the most by CBOE's trading pit. Although the size diminished significantly due to electronic trading, people were still making gestures and shouting out the price of their orders, as we saw in movies and news. It is disappointing that all financial companies visiting this time prohibit us from taking photos, leaving no pictures behind.

- Federal Reserve Bank of Chicago

As one of the 12 Federal Reserve Bank, Chicago is responsible for the Midwest grain belt areas of Illinois, Indiana, Michigan, Wisconsin, and Iowa. At the Money Museum inside the bank, we looked at the circulation process and heard an explanation of the role of the central bank. The Federal Reserve said its main task is to properly manage interest rates and control unemployment by controlling the money supply.

The night view of Chicago

- CTC (Chicago Trading Company)

  It is a leading trading company in Chicago. A graduate of the University of Illinois engineering is CEO. The CEO greets him and the head quant, Dr. Greg Sobczak, gave a lecture. It is a prop trading company that deals only with equity and deals mainly with options. It has offices in Chicago and London.

- CME Group (Chicago Mercantile Exchange & Chicago Board of Trade)

  CME is Chicago's flagship options and futures exchange, and the company looked substantial. After merging CBOT in 2007, they became the CME group. After completing the necessary explanations and Q&A, we went down to the exchange and saw the actual trading room, but it had a large number of monitors like CTC. I received a business card from the person in charge, and it said this on the title: "CME is where futures are made." It means CME is the place where futures contracts are made, and I also could catch the hidden meaning of it.

- CBOE (Chicago Board Options Exchange)

  If CME is a futures exchange, CBOE is an exchange that specializes in options. CBOE was established in 1973 by CBOT and seemed to have had considerable friction within CBOT over the equity issue with CBOT. Everything became electronic, and there was only one trading floor left, at which dealers and market makers shouted. Everything has implemented into a trading system, and in the future, it will eventually be a technology firm like Goldman Sachs.

  The middle-aged female market maker who educated us was impressive. Currently, male employees here are said to be in their 60s and women in their 20s. She seemed to be in her late fifties, and she explained the history of the U.S. exchange honestly and interestingly in terms of her career changes. Also, she hinted about the problems she felt working with the smart Ph.D. Quants.

- Blockchains and Cryptocurrencies

  'Annual financial engineering colloquium' opened in Chicago Illini Center. There were four speakers. Dr. Andrew Miller (UIUC ECE professor) was a man who received his Ph.D. in blockchain and appeared to be onto it in the future. A female business lecturer from CME demonstrated her outstanding capacity to present with the Bible as the motif based on his profound experiences and knowledge.

  Bitcoin is cryptocurrency based on blockchain technology, and it was developed by a man named Satoshi Nakamoto in 2009. Bitcoin is a peer-to-peer currency that has no physical form and no managing body. Bitcoin is made by a process called mining, and the blockchain is a public ledger, which records a bitcoin transaction, and thus cannot be hacked because it is stored on nodes around the world.

Thanksgiving and parking fine of $50

Since Puritans who emigrated from England founded the United States, the culture of Christianity is deeply rooted in this society, and Thanksgiving is one of them. Thanksgiving Day in the United States falls on the fourth Thursday of November every year, but universities are closed for the entire week due to the holidays.

Students start the fall semester at the end of August and are already exhausted by the end of November, the Thanksgiving holiday, so they have a rest during the holiday and then again burning their final sparks in the final exam of mid-December.

Likewise, a week's spring break will be given in mid-March right after the midterm exam.

Sadly, however, I had to spend most of this Thanksgiving holiday writing the secondary research paper, the primary assignment of the academic writing class. On Monday, I drove to the engineering library to do it, and I mistook it was a holiday, but a few hours later I found a ticket issued and pressed under the windshield wiper. It seems that the official holidays at school are only for Thursdays and Fridays. That's why Monday was the day of the parking control, and they found my car, which was parked without a permit.

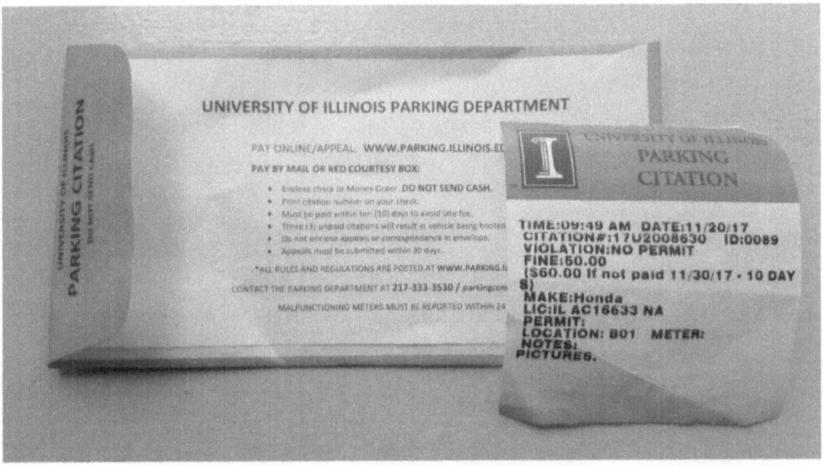

University of Illinois parking citation

My wife couldn't afford a dollar at ALDI mart, so I was heartbroken because I was going to lose 50 dollars. On the other hand, I feel that life is fleeting: 50 dollars is not a lot of money compared to tuition and there is no point in saving on eating at the market when we think about the changes in the value of stocks a day.

Parking fines seem to be a source of income for the school. It was well-made on a web page to make it easier to pay for a single bank transfer. The school's parking system categorized into two areas: a coin-parkable area and an area where annual parking tickets are to be purchased. Coin parking areas can be parked free of charge on weekends and holidays or after 5 p.m. on weekdays. Coin parking costs 15 minutes per quarter or one hour per dollar, and we can pay through a mobile app called 'Pay by Phone.'

School gym, ARC and CRCE

There are several sports facilities throughout the school, including an indoor soccer field and tennis courts, but ARC and CRCE are the two most representative indoor sports facilities. Both have Indoor running tracks, as well as indoor training facilities and swimming pools so that you can run in the middle of winter or the rain. ARC track is a quarter mile around, CRCE is one-eighth of a mile.

Warm-up is proper in five minutes with stretching, and after running for 30 minutes in earnest, the rowing machine cools down to 1,000 meters and finishes. The direction of the

ARC 2nd floor indoor track

running track showed on a sign, but it was a little awkward because it was clockwise last time, but today it was turned counterclockwise.

Students can always use the gym within their operating hours because the tuition includes the gym fare. And there are many password temporary set-up lockers like the library so that you can store simple items such as bags easily. However, a regular cabinet in a swimming pool or shower facility must be carried by an individual with a lock.

There's an indoor rock-climbing facility, but I'm not sure if I will use it. When I was a university student, I once went to an indoor rock climbing in Gangnam, Seoul. I remember that my body was heavy, and arm strength was lacking, so my feet were fluttering when I climbed high.

Indoor rock climbing

1.2 English: Missing Half of Listening

Missing half of listening

If people talk slowly, considering me as a foreigner, I can understand most of the time, but when they speak, as usual, it was hard to understand even half of them. What the professor says in class is mostly understandable if I go to the classroom prepared, or I seem to miss half of it. In other words, with some background knowledge, I can guess a little bit and understand a lot, but without background knowledge, I have to rely only on pure listening skills, and in this case, I miss a lot.

The importance of listening

Speaking is important, but first of all, if the listening isn't right, it's a disaster. People care about me as a foreigner once or twice, but if I don't get it over and over again, no one will feel good about it. Once I wanted to visit a professor at the office hours for some advice on my paper, but I couldn't understand him. His words were not clear, and his voice was small, making them difficult for most students to understand. But American students seemed to understand most of the time.

On the other hand, I want to participate in class, such as questions, but I am not confident in listening and speaking. And it was almost impossible to understand what other classmates were saying or asking questions. That's because students ask questions in a small voice, and I am not used to Chinese and Indian accents, which makes me even harder to get it.

I don't know what kind of luck the Americans, the U.K., and Australians enjoy just by speaking their language. If they were born as Koreans in their next life, I would feel better watching them experiencing a similar situation to me.

My wife and I feel that it is impossible to speak English as jokingly as Americans do now, even though we live in the U.S. for 20 years. Our goal is to become a 'bilingual' between Korean and English so that we can understand everything people say in English and we can speak what we want to say comfortably in English.

Robot English tutor

In my field of experience, the most promising areas in the future are robot stock advisors and robot English tutors. I wish I could keep practicing one-on-one with a good English teacher, but it would be too expensive and practically impossible. As an alternative, I need an artificial intelligence English speaking robot that I can practice with while continuing my dialog with the robot. Currently, the smartphone application on the market is hardly useful.

And if this method is impossible anyway, I think it's best to train English alone. We can do image training in daily life. "One keyword and one sentence explaining the keyword why you think so is enough."

I do not change my opinion that reading is the most important thing. Text reading has a massive impact on listening, speaking, and writing. Listening affects speaking and writing. And speaking affects writing. Finally, writing has the smallest impact on other areas and is relatively independent. In other words, if you think about the English learning phase as a

Second Language, it is sequentially reading, listening, speaking, and writing.

Xfinity cable broadcasting

The cable supply vendor here in the graduate family dormitory is Comcast's Xfinity, and I can watch with a smartphone or laptop without a TV. After getting a refund on TV at Walmart last time, I didn't repurchase it. The reason for this is that Taeju watches exotic programs all day long.

U.S. cable channels have too many commercials in between. I often watch HLN, FS1, and CNN. HLN is a separate broadcast from CNN, short for Headline News. Korean-American football player Hines Ward was also on a panel at a wake-up news program.

Forensic files were the best thing for me to watch, and HLN broadcasted it every evening. Narrator, Peter Thomas is a legendary American announcer who died in 2014, and the voice of the Forensics file was said to be irreplaceable by anyone. My wife said his voice was similar to Kim Sang-Joong in 'Unanswered Questions.' There are about 400 episodes until season 14, but there is a problem that it keeps playing what I saw the other day.

Reading English newspapers

University is offering free newspapers for students in libraries, dormitories, and other areas of the school. Or, more precisely, the tuition includes this cost. Therefore, newspapers are not offered during the break.

There are three kinds of newspapers: USA Today, New York Times, and Chicago Tribune. Among them, I bring the New

York Times and the Chicago Tribune, see them, and hand them over to my house. I only read about 15 minutes a day during lunch in the library, but my wife reads for many hours at home. Skimming solely focuses on the title, but it has the effect of knowing how the world is going and somehow feels knowledgeable.

Reading the headlines in the New York Times at lunch time

When I studied GRE, I wondered where these difficult words could have a use, but there were a lot of GRE words appearing in actual English newspapers, and I often looked in the materials related to my major classes.

Thoughts on how to train English

I also listened to a YouTube program called 'Live Academy (LA in short) during the winter break. It was a broadcast where my wife praised for being excellent, and I was looking for some source to study English from now on. I hardly studied English in this first semester. I was so caught up in school homework and exams, and then only I could share a few words of life English that I needed. I can't help but feel that my English is getting backward because there are only math and statistics in my head.

A scene from the Live Academy video

My idea about English training is that it is best to memorize things that apply to me by hand. No matter how much good the Live Academy tells me, I don't think I can use it when it's in a hurry without organizing it in my way. No matter how much I take a video lecture for my discipline all day, it is like I can't have a test well unless I read it and organize it in my head. And basically, the best way to study is to pick out good content and memorize it. In the process of memorization, people naturally understand it.

1.3 Life: Car-Centric Country

Housing

The most significant cost of studying in the U.S. besides tuition is rent for a house. Fortunately, Midwest here is less than half of New York or L.A. although rentals still the most significant fixed expenditure. Squirrels here can live well on trees at minus 30 degrees Celsius, but people can't stand a night without a home. Especially if you have children, the importance of a home where you can rest comfortably will be all the more essential.

The graduate family dormitory here is called an apartment building, but in fact, it is close to a townhouse with a long two-story building on its side. There are also many price differences depending on the location of buildings and whether the furniture is provided, the number of rooms, or remodeling.

Graduate family housing at Orchard Downs

We have a two-bedroom, furnished and remodeled apartment, and we pay rent about $900 a month. Since the building itself is more than 30 to 40 years old, existing buildings other than remodeling are not durable to cold and noise and have to walk around the laundry room even in the middle of winter. Utility costs, such as electricity, gas, and water, appear to be around $90 a month on average.

Forest view from my home

Our building, in particular, has the college arboretum right in front of it, so I like the forest view. A little further from the side is the Japan House, which is a dating course for University of Illinois students.

Urbana is a typical U.S. middle-class residential area where houses have their place neatly. By comparison, Champaign is somewhat commercial and close to school, where many young unmarried students reside. The city, called Savoy, is also close to the south, and although public transportation is a little inconvenient, it is a preferred area for Korean families because of its good school district and right living conditions such as the mart. Students and their families will reside in one of these three cities.

Eating and Living

Here is a small town, a couple of hours' drives from a nearby metropolis, but most of the infrastructure, including schools, supermarkets, hospitals, and government offices, is well-established, so it is not a problem to eat and live. It is the most significant difference from South Korea, which is hard to live in the countryside, as all of its infrastructures are concentrated in the Seoul area.

The U.S. is a paradise for large marts including Meijer, Walmart, ALDI, and Schnucks. ALDI has a meager price. Eggs cost about 50 cents for a dozen and a dollar for a gallon of milk. Meijer and Walmart are also cheap and nice, but as they're so big, it takes a lot of time to shop, and it's hard to catch kids running around like crazy. Based on Germany, ALDI is a global chain with about 10,000 stores in 20 countries, including Europe, the United States and Australia, and about 2,000 in the U.S.

Urbana ALDI mart in the middle of winter

Meijer, on the other hand, is an American chain where Dutch immigrants started in Michigan, mostly in the Midwest, including Michigan, Illinois, Kansas, Wisconsin, and Ohio. After all, since there are not many things to eat out in the U.S. and they are so expensive, buying ingredients at a mart is an essential part of our life, and my wife is busy cooking for breakfast and dinner.

Meanwhile, there is also a Korean mart called AM-KO in Champaign. It appears that a Korean woman and her American husband operate together, and we come by when we need Korean side dishes such as kimchi, bean sprouts, and soybean paste, although the size is not very large. The mart is located in the Champaign midtown, and it is used not only by Koreans but also by various races. It seemed to offer black bananas for free, as shown in the picture. I can't forget the face of a black lady who was picking something to eat from among those bananas when I first went. She looked very poor, but she was smiling and seemed to have bananas to feed her children.

Bananas at AM-KO Korean Mart

Car-centric country

While Western Europe is a bicycle-oriented country, the U.S. is all about a car-oriented culture. The house is all built with a driveway in front of it. Cars are an essential part of American life where land is vast, and public transportation is not dense. It is often too far to walk nearby due to the sparse number of houses, and when the sun sets, it is dark and deserted, making it scary to walk.

I went to the U.S. after I made an appointment to buy one of the cars on the Korean Student Association website here. For those who study abroad or return home after studying abroad, dealing with the car sale is the most critical and annoying thing. It takes time to sell because of its large size and not a penny, and it also involves car registration and insurance. And if you don't know your car well, you can be fooled or damaged, so it bothers you.

Fortunately, I am grateful to former car owner Jang Se-Hyun for letting me purchase a right used car (Honda CR-V 2013) at an affordable price. I heard that he came here with his family for a year of research as a doctoral researcher at Hyundai Motor company. I feel sorry for my car as a new owner because I don't think I can manage the car so clean. Anyway, I used the car every day for the first two months. I went to school and came home around 6 o'clock, ate dinner, drove back to the school library. It's impossible without a car. My car was named 'Black Honda.'

My car was insured in American Family Insurance, suggested by the church person who helped me settle down. Considering the case of an accident, I joined the recommended Korean agent as it would be difficult to explain the situation in an emergency. In Korea, I paid about $350 a year for the insurance premium. For here, I signed up for it every six months, and the premium was very high though I have proof of my safe driving career in Korea. If it expires this time, I will consider direct insurance, like 'Progressive.'

Department of Motor Vehicle (DMV) is responsible for vehicle registration and driver's license issuance in the United States. My car registration was done at the Rantoul DMV, 25 minutes away, and I liked there because it was so fast and friendly.

DMV in Rantoul, IL

Unfortunately, however, if you don't have a social security number (SSN), you won't be able to take a driver's test there. To deal with a person who does not have an SSN, some information must have arrived from the administrative headquarters, but small DMV doesn't seem to be able to do it.

Used car acquisition and vehicle registration

When signing and acquiring a used car, it is better to write a simple contract on a blank sheet of paper, even for personal transactions. In the agreement, you can write down the VIN, title no, mileage and sales amount, and a sign of the seller/buyer.

After the purchase of the vehicle, you must have an insurance policy to register the car with the DMV. You can contact the insurance agent in advance, send the necessary documents, arrange them, and contact them as soon as the purchase contract is signed and receive the insurance certificate by smartphone.

And when a seller signs up for the car title he had at the time of registration and submits it to DMV, they give you a new license plate, and the new title is later mailed out. Existing license plates can be replaced and discarded. The car title, written on red paper, is also referred to as 'pink slip.'

The self-service gas station

In Korea, there are often self-fueling stations, but here I have never seen a place that is not a self-service gas station. Anyway, I'm still not used to refueling. Sometimes it doesn't work well because of my fault or its inferior machines. Then, I have to open the gas cap of the car first and manipulate the card payment. If I pay first, open the lid, select the oil, and dawdle, I'll have to start over again. If this is repeated two or three times, the card will be locked for security reasons. "Please see cashier."

Self-fueling of 87 octane gasoline

All gas stations are with convenience stores, and if you have any questions, you should go into the convenience store and talk. Gasoline is about $2.5 per gallon, which is very cheap compared to Korea, so it costs about $30 to fill it up. There are usually three gas grades to choose from, but I put the cheapest one, octane 87. According to the manual of the vehicle, there is a minimum octane requirement, which is usually 87.

Driver's license

I planned to buy a used car in the U.S. and get my U.S. driver's license first, but I couldn't get it right away with an F-1 visa. The license acquisition basis for F-1 student is I-20, which is said to be ten days after the start of the semester when I-20 has been finalized and is valid for the whole operation. I checked it on the Champaign DMV and found that my I-20 was not entered in the computer system. I learned this by asking the school ISSS to inquire. I found many things on the Internet before I went to the U.S., but I am disappointed that there was no such information anywhere.

Under Illinois law, a driver's license in a foreign country (including an international driver's license) or other state was only valid for three months, so I had to go early in the morning to line up at DMV every Saturday. Auto insurance premiums have become more expensive for international licenses. Anyway, it has been inconvenient to come to take a license test, especially during the busy school year.

The process of obtaining a driver's license from the Champaign DMV is a real curse. The written test passed quickly with the brochures provided by DMV. The problem is that there are so many people who want to take the road test all day. I've been there every Saturday morning, but I've been wasting my time trying to find all the turn. In the end, I was able to get inside the line one day, but I should wait almost five hours to take the road test.

The infamous Champaign DMV

The first road test supervisor was a slightly older grandpa. He severely admonished people like me who were not familiar with the road for missing the stop sign. I felt terrible. I finally passed my second road test a week later, but then I was scolded by another supervisor. I was embarrassed because I missed his English a few times.

The major difference between driving a car in the U.S. and Korea is that every left turn contains an unprotected turn, so you have to turn left if you don't have a car coming to you on the green light. Turning right is similar to Korea, but if the signal ahead is red, you should stop just like the one with a stop sign and turn right after looking for any priority vehicles.

And you need to get into the habit of driving by looking at the street sign rather than the navigation device. Otherwise, it is easy to miss the road when the test supervisor orders you to turn left on the next street or turn right at the next intersection. And, using maps and milestones is useful in many ways to drive with the outline of the entire road in your head. Navigation is only for reference purposes.

If you pass the road test, you can take pictures of your upper body and print out a piece of paper that corresponds to a temporary license. The driver's license, which arrived in the mail two weeks later, was not available for use as an identification card, and its expiration date was not long because it follows the dates on I-20.

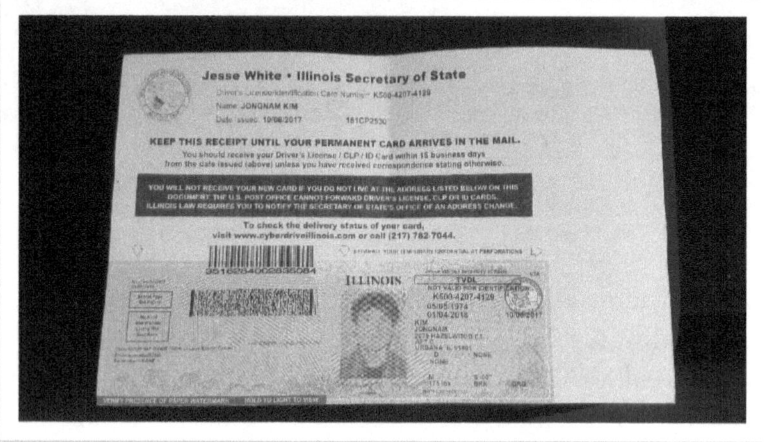

Temporary license issued after passing the road test

Anyway, I think getting a license as an F-1 status is a lot of trouble in many ways. I forgot for a moment that I was not a resident of this country but a 'temporary visitor.'

Cell phone, Internet

There is a cell phone shop run by a Korean, named 'Blink Mobile' on Green Street. Its primary carrier is H2O, which is MVNO. Does it mean, like water, it's indispensable? It uses AT&T network and costs $27 a month. It's a $30 unlimited plan, and if you pay automatically, you get with $27 and your data is limited by one gigabyte a month.

You can make unlimited phone calls to Korea on five phone numbers every month, but in my case, I don't have much to use. Make a call to Korea is in order of 011, followed by Korea National Code (82), Area Code, and Telephone Number. For example, 011-82-2-10-2345-6789 like that.

In the case of MVNO, additional settings are required to use the MMS. SMS is not a problem. There is a way to make MMS possible if you look on the Internet, but I am just using SMS. Also, when I call my wife, I often have to dial twice without being able to connect at once. It seems that there are many places where cell phone signals are weak in the U.S.

Comcast's cable service, Xfinity provide the Internet, and my apartment rental fee already includes it. Xfinity's stream service is accessible from TVs, smartphones, Kindle, and other devices and can only be accessed concurrently by one person per household. I recently received mail saying that my Internet service can connect to five devices at the same time by bandwidth doubling from 25 Mbps to 60 Mbps. I called technical services, but they confirmed that only one person could access them simultaneously with the ID assigned to the school apartment.

Comcast technical service visited our home

Postal service

The United States has a short, easy-to-work address system, and basically, all contacts come through the mail. Mailboxes are jointly located in front of an apartment, and what's unique is the way the slightly larger parcels are received. There is a somewhat large locker at the bottom of the mailbox, and the postman puts the key in the mailbox of the home where the parcel is received, and we use that key to open and receive the large package. Once we've picked the key, we can't take it out again, so it prevents the loss of the key. I didn't know this way, so I contacted Amazon because I didn't have the item I ordered, and I found out that I had to open my mailbox.

Laptop computer, Best Buy, and Amazon

The Toshiba notebook that I took from Korea accidently broke down, so I stopped by Champaign Best Buy that evening. It is hard to live without a laptop because there is programming homework every week.

Apartment mailbox

Best Buy is an offline store famous for its electronics products, but it seems to me that it is much cheaper to use Amazon online. Amazon offers free Prime services to university students for six months, and in terms of price and service, it is unlikely that any other company will beat the Amazon.

Best Buy store in Champaign, IL

And there was a technical problem with the laptop connector of the car's jump starter, so I contacted both the Best Bye and Lenovo, saying they don't know, and Amazon, the vendor of the jump starter, was in charge until the end. They offered 10-dollar discounts. Amazon's customer service was remarkably thorough. Once camping mattress was broken because my daughter had jumped on it. I asked for repairs on Amazon, but they were willing to refund it. There seems to be a reason why Amazon has grown this way.

Anyway, the product I bought at Best Buy on that day was Lenovo Yoga 710-15IKB. It's a 2-in-1 notebook with a 15.6-inch screen. It can be touched on the screen and can be folded and used as a tablet. I chose a rather heavy laptop with a big screen to watch PDF books. Overall, I am satisfied, but I often make

LENOVO YOGA 710-15IKB notebook

typos when I write in Korean because the right shift key is smaller than the left one. It will take time to get used to it.

November, Illinois

I've heard a lot about the cold weather here, but it's still okay. Instead, October was quite cold and is now warmer than Seoul. However, it is also scary to hear that the sun is getting shorter and it's dark at 4 pm in the winter.

There are no mountains in Illinois, so the wind from Lake Michigan is quite strong. The rain also hit the side, and the umbrella is not useful. But the sky is clear and high so that I can see the trajectory of the airplane flying in the air very high.

Most of all, this is the heaven of squirrels. Where did squirrels store acorns for winter? It seems to me that the squirrels here don't make any extra effort to save. As there are so many acorns in the trees and they fall off, it will spread out even in winter.

Sunset of November

White Christmas and battery discharge

December 23th, 2017. Snowy snow first came. I woke up on Saturday morning, and it was all white outside the window. My family sleeps past midnight watching TV on their cell phones or tablets these days. I often wake up late because I have winter break for a month, but my wife wakes up early in the morning. Her own time in the early morning would be invaluable because kids always interrupt her when they are awake.

I jogged through the snowy Arboretum forest. The snow was very gentle, but it's only the beginning of severe winter.

The next day, Christmas Eve, Sunday morning, the snow was heavy. I ate a quick breakfast and started the car to go to church, but I couldn't catch it at all. It's been a week of car rides, and there's been a lot of voltage drop in cold weather all night. The car's battery starts with 12 to 10 volts, but it is now estimated to be around 6-7 volts. The morning temperature was minus 4 degrees, but it fell to minus 14 degrees overnight.

Inevitably, we gave up going to church and called the insurance company to get a jump service.

Emergency service vehicle came from a nearby private car center signed with an insurance company. It's not an ignorant way to carry a large car battery, but it takes a second for a small auxiliary battery to connect it to my cell and start it up.

Taye and my wife in the snow

My wife and children love it because it snowed a lot. Our lower house, Angel's family headed for the Arboretum hill with a snow sled.

Full-scale winter

Seoul is also cold in winter, but it is easy here to be minus 20 degrees Celsius in the morning. It was minus 19 degrees this morning, and next week it's forecasted to be below minus 25 degrees. According to HLN broadcasts, the Arctic cold air has come down. It must have been frozen all night long since I felt the heater turning on often. The heater automatically starts at 68 degrees Fahrenheit (20 degrees Celsius) in my house.

The Midwest here, including Chicago, is said to be a cold area that sometimes goes below minus 30 degrees Celsius in winter, but it was not very cold in early 2017. However, it is freezing in early 2018. There was also a windstorm in the east, and the cars covered with ice like the Disney animation 'Frozen.'

The forest of Arboretum from my house in winter

The car won't start because many days are around minus 20 degrees. The battery was not new, but there was nothing wrong with using it in summer and fall, and it seems that charging does not produce enough voltage to start it in this weather.

I bought a jump starter from Amazon and used it when I don't get started, considering the way I got the jump service from the insurance company last time. I bought it for $75. In addition to the 12-volt car jump, it has the ability of power bank to charge my laptop (19-volt output), cell phone, and other devices. That is, I bought it with the intention of summer camping in mind.

When the weather gets warmer, I'll check the performance and replace the battery myself if necessary, with a 10-millimeter

Jump starter, connected to the car battery

wrench and pliers at the market. In Korea, I have a set of car-tools that I used to use, but I left them because they were heavy. About 15 minutes is expected for replacement as I'm unskilled.

My wife has had my haircut twice

It's Christmas Eve. It is my second haircut since I came to America. There's nowhere to go for it, and my wife did the same thing last time. She put the newspaper on the floor of our living room and cut it off with paper scissors.

Last time, I felt like my back hair was a bit long and she cut more hairs on my left, so I hinted at two things this time. Anyway, I think she did a good job, and I'm satisfied.

Dental treatment for my wife

My wife has many teeth that have been treated since she was young. She thinks there's a genetic effect. Anyway, I heard that one of her teeth broke a little while cleaning a month ago, but she is quite anxious because yesterday the tooth broke more while eating. I am also worried that dental care is too expensive in the U.S. However, it's rotten and broken, so there is no pain yet.

She has two options: find affordable dentistry here or go to Korea to get treatment. It looks like about 20 percent of the tooth is rotten and broken, but it should be decided which treatment is appropriate among the filling or root canal treatment.

I found it on the bulletin board of the Korean Student Association and asked a Korean dentist here. It costs 80 dollars only to check and get an estimate, and it would be two to three thousand dollars if she had root canal treatment. Root canal therapy is expensive in the United States, and there is a separate doctor. The cost of implants is around $2,000 to $3,000 for necessary treatments alone, and the cost of materials is additional.

After several phone calls and visits, a call came from a Champaign local dental program called 'Smile Healthy.' It is a social security dental program that is given a particular discount according to the income level, a common way in American society. We eventually decided to receive treatment for resin filling there. The doctor appeared to be a young volunteer and recommended a root canal treatment and crown, but my wife had chosen to fill it out because root canal cost more than $2,000 and took a long time. She saw the X-ray, and it wasn't as big as she thought it would be. Anyway, when she returns to Korea, I think she needs to do the additional treatment.

Twin City Bible Church (TCBC)

My wife and I have the Protestant faith. In Korea, we regularly went to church together in the early days of marriage, but we didn't go well after we had a baby. There are many Korean churches in the U.S., but we wanted to experience many things during our short stay, so we visited an American church near our house, Twin City Bible Church (TCBC), located in Urbana. I liked the calm and family atmosphere, and I loved it even better because I saw someone I happened to know before.

Twin City Bible Church in Urbana, IL

The person I ran into at the church is Mr. Keach, who volunteers for the lending room in our graduate family housing. He said he immigrated from Japan to the U.S. at an early age, graduated from college in the U.S. and worked in an IT-related job for 30 years in the Chicago area before settling down here after retirement. He lives with his old mother and looks like he has no children. He has a quiet personality, but he seems to be friendly and warm.

Keach happened to see us in church and introduced us to David. He was a great man who has been running Friday night's Bible study at his own home for more than 35 years. He invited us to the Bible study.

Having attended several services, it seems that the American Church is more likely to be voluntarily operated by the volunteers. And the structure of the chapel is at its lowest point. A pastor does not always do a sermon, and sometimes, other Christians give a speech instead of the pastor.

Sunday morning worship service

It is particularly helpful because the church provides child care while adults are at worship service. Several rooms are separated by age, and the church members seem to be taking care of as a volunteer. At first, I was happy for them to take care of my kids, but as time goes by, I felt a little sorry and uncomfortable about just receiving it.

Friday night Bible study

Church activity is now a big part of our American social life. There is a Bible study meeting on weekdays as well as Sunday, so my wife and I are participating. I was taking Taeju to a Bible study on Friday evening, but I could hardly go by the end of the semester because the deadline for my programming assignment is midnight every Friday. Besides Sunday, Ruth, David's wife, also holds a women's meeting at the church on weekdays.

The Bible study is held every Friday, 7 p.m. at David & Ruth's home, and David drives a 15-seat van himself, providing rides. In recent years, the number of Chinese studying in the U.S. has soared, and they are becoming primary targets of American missionary work due to the small number of Christians among Chinese. In David's Bible study, Chinese students, scholars, and their families are the absolute majority.

David & Ruth family

David and Ruth had seven children, and it seemed that only one of them had married. David graduated from an MBA at the University of Illinois and has long worked as a faculty member here at the school. In the process, he has been running the Bible study with his wife Ruth for more than 30 years, and later quit school and work full-time as an international student missionary for the International Student Institute (ISI).

Bible, the best seller in the world

I've been to church from childhood to adulthood, but I don't think I've read the Bible correctly. It is better to read the Bible with an easy English book written for children. In particular, 'Adventure Bible,' which TCBC gave me to read Taeju, is also suitable for adults because of its well-described explanation for each chapter. And its English is easy to understand as it is an NIV (NIrV) version. Taeju likes the book because it has a 3D cover, and Taye likes it because the car comes out in the cover.

Children Bible getting from TCBC

1.4 Parenting: Kids Increase Entropy

Nature of raising children

I think the child grows up on its own, and the parents are a helper. It is similar to the night-watchman state theory, and parents want to support only the minimum amount of assistance, such as the safety of their children and watch and help their children grow up on their own. Also, it is hard to do anymore because a child is a person and does not work as I wish.

The reality is tough. As I have to study and do my homework at the library on weekends, I feel sorry for leaving my house with my wife and children left. Children do not sit still for a moment while they are awake. I wanted to let them play on their own in the front yard, but the housing community stopped even that.

Most children don't try to play alone but ask their parents to keep playing with them. There are also times when it is dangerous to leave it alone. My wife was having a hard time because I could only help her once in a while. In Korea, my mother-in-law and father-in-law took care of the children, so I didn't know it was hard, but I'm feeling it right now. I realize now how hard they must have had to take care of my children.

There is a dangerous item for children among the furniture provided in this apartment. It fell twice and almost got in trouble. Once Taeju, once Taye. It's enough to hurt a child badly if it's laid down there. I once got my wife's phone call from the library at midnight. Taye opened the closet and played with it, and the cabinet fell, and he was laid a little under it.

The heavy wooden wardrobe

Due to the nature of the wardrobe, if he opens a few drawers and hangs them there, he might be able to focus his weight on the principle of leverage. It is sturdy wooden furniture that can never be knocked over if used usually, but our children are second to none. When I went home and cleaned up, I thought it was fortunate. I prayed to God, and the closet changed its layout so that it could get caught on a wall or a desk.

Vaccination for school admission

Before I came here to study, I had a hard time getting the immunity required by the university. I would have received most of the vaccinations when I was young, but I had no memory, no records, and no one used a parenting diary in those days. I ended up getting vaccinated again. For the TDP, which has to be injected three times, the last one was at a school health center in the United States. In the case of Korea, for people born after the 2000s, like our children, all vaccinations records are computerized, and you can quickly issue in a local health center.

There were three essential immunizations required by the University of Illinois. Other schools in the U.S. would be similar.

First is MMR (Measles-Mumps-Rubella). The second is TDP (Tetanus-Diphtheria-Pertussis), which must be inoculated three times in total, one of which must be Tdap. Here, Tdap's 'a' stands for 'acellular' and is known to be more expensive but effective, and it is not possible to be under the age of seven. Finally, the Meningococcal Conjugate Vaccine is that. It only requires 16 to 21-year-olds.

Champaign-Urbana Public Health District

To enter elementary school, Taeju also had to submit vaccination records and undergo dental and eye examinations. It was easy thanks to bringing both vaccination and dental records from Korea in English. One thing is that chicken pox was popular in the U.S. several years ago, so children should also get chicken pox vaccinations. Fortunately, children were given the necessary checkups at Champaign-Urbana Public Health District at a low price.

Dr. Martin Luther King, Jr. Elementary School

The elementary school where Taeju entered is Martin Luther King, Jr. Elementary School, short for King School. Dr. King, who led the American civil rights movement in the 1950s and 1960s, won the Nobel Peace Prize in 1964.

Although Taeju is only five years old and is in kindergarten age, it is the beginning grade of an elementary school in the U.S. That is why she entered elementary school. The public education system in the United States is called K-12 (from K-grade to 12-grade), where K stands for Kindergarten. Middle school is three years from 6th to 8th grade, and high school education is usually four years, which is 9th to 12th grade.

The day to enter King School, Taeju disappeared somewhere

The King School is located in the northern part of Urbana and is home to a large number of black people. It is a school with ESL classes, so it is necessary for children who are not familiar with English to go through it. There are also many children of Chinese students, so there was even a separate class of them. However, it is hard to find Korean students. Korean mothers, sensitive to education, left for Savoy and other places in search of good school districts, instead of leaving them in such ordinary public education schools. Chinese mothers prefer schools with fewer Chinese because their educational zeal is also high. So, King school is getting more and more black students' school. However, it's still happy to see the clear eyes of black children.

In the classroom where Taeju is going to study

King was actually born in a wealthy family, and his father was also a pastor. He tried to become a lawyer, but he eventually studied theology at his father's suggestion, and I think he experienced a lot of discrimination in college because he was black. Later, he became a pastor and began a campaign for black human rights and made his name known to the world as a boycott of Montgomery buses. A black woman was arrested on a bus in Alabama for refusing to give up her seat to a white man, a ridiculous incident that now seems to be happening.

King campaigned nonviolently for equal human rights of black people and was deeply remembered by the world for his famous speech, which began with "I have a dream" in 1963. His influence on Americans at the time was so significant that the FBI kept him in extreme surveillance. Eventually, King was assassinated in 1968 by a figure from a radical white group. Later in the U.S., around King's birthday, January 15, it was honored as a federal holiday by designating the third Monday of January as Martin Luther King, Jr. Day.

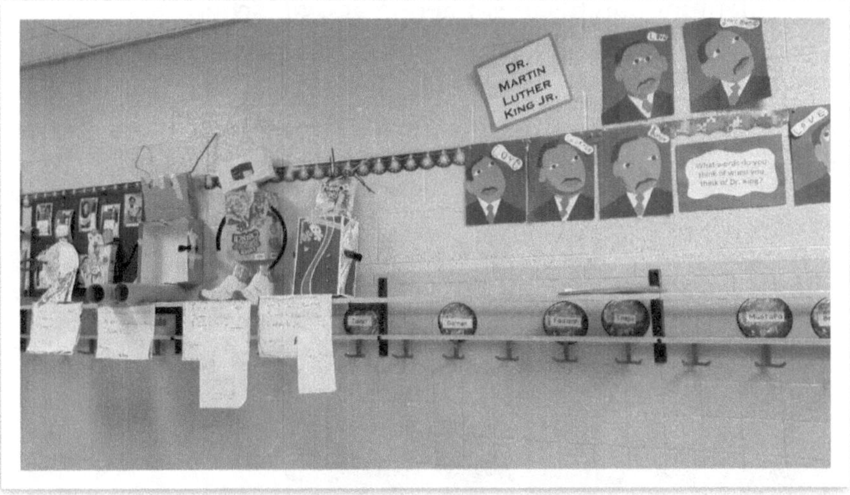

The entrance to the Taeju's classroom

Taeju's suffering in the United States

For a girl, Taeju is very energetic and almost boyish, but she is an adorable daughter to look at her face. These days, Taeju is suffering from stress (growth pains) while adapting to public education in the U.S.

First, she is having a hard time with English. In Korea, she enjoyed speaking because she learned to talk early. In American schools, her listening is just understandable, and speaking is poor. Many adults say, "Don't worry about children. They can adapt to English very quickly." But I think they don't know well because they haven't experienced it before. Sometimes when we talk about Korea during a conversation, she asks me to send her back to kindergarten in Korea, and my heart aches.

Secondly, Taeju's public education is as long as adults. At 7:30 in the morning, she takes a school bus and comes back at 3:30 in the afternoon, and we send her back to the after-school program at the Community Center by 5:30. It is very convenient for parents to get her on and off school buses because the community center is in front of our home. However, it seems that the social life of Taeju is almost as long as I do, so if she feels tired sometimes, we let her come home and rest without after school.

Orchard Downs Community Center

One day, Mrs. Puffer called my wife from King School and asked her to take the test, so my wife was worried. Mrs. Puffer thought there might be a problem with the sensory system, saying that Taeju kept walking back and forth without sitting still at school and taking her hands around face often. Then, she asked a professional teacher to have Taeju examined. In my opinion, it is a level of behavior for children of that age, but I think Mrs. Puffer probably had some misunderstanding because Taeju didn't understand the teacher's English well. Anyway, we agreed to the test and observed it for a long time, but we also paid more attention to Taeju and have not had any problems since.

On the last Friday of October, we went to school because there was a conference day between parents and teachers. I went to Taeju's school, saw the teacher again, and played with Taye in the school playground. Mrs. Puffer estimated that Taeju has good English listening but doesn't want to speak well. Anyway, it's a good thing that Taeju likes her teacher.

Children increase entropy

There is the second law of thermodynamics that entropy in the universe always moves in an increasing direction. Entropy is often understood as 'measure of disorder,' and it is like the anarchy that occurs when trees burn and become ash. The first law of thermodynamics preserves the entire energy, but the second law increases entropy.

Unlike adults, the child seems to feel more comfortable in the distractions than in order. As time goes by, entropy increases, which is the law of nature. Adults feel comfortable with being organized by artificial energy applied to it, but children are glad to follow nature's regimen.

No matter how much you clean your house, it's no use, and after an hour or two, it turns into a dump. Taye starts when he plays with everything in the box upside down. From an adult's point of view, it's hard to understand. When he spilled milk by accident, he seems to be happy to rub it again with hands. He likes vacuum cleaners very much, and once a day, he opens the vacuum cleaner's canister and pours the dust from it onto the carpet.

Jumping like a monkey in a bed is Taeju's hobby and winter exercise. No matter what parents say, it's just then, and no matter how much we say it, she doesn't listen. It's my baby, but I wonder how those kids came out.

Kids love smartphones, tablets

The relationship between the child and the parent is the same as the one between the sun and the earth, so a proper distance is needed. In other words, too much attention hinders a child's independence and makes the parents tired themselves. However, given the children's interest and concentration on smartphones and tablets, it seems to be addictive if left to the free will.

Taeju, Taye loves going to the mart. They like it more than the playground because they can drive with mom and dad and run around in lots of places to eat and see. Walmart is so big that there are so many things to tempt children that parents are hard to do. So, we prefer small mart like ALDI.

However, it's a cold winter now, so kids seem to prefer watching tablets in a warm house to going to the mart. Children can watch their smartphones or tablets without ever taking their eyes off until the battery runs out. Tests show that the eyes of a StarCraft game player were rarely blinked when observed with a camera, which is abnormal and very unhealthy.

Adults can hardly escape the temptation of smartphones, but children are almost impossible on their own free will. Kids try to watch the tablet even during mealtime, so I'm teaching them to turn it off and rest during mealtime, though it's their freedom to eat or not. Adults should reduce their children's tablet use to a minimum and talk to them a lot — not only the child but also the wife.

Jealousy for her younger brother

Although Taeju likes her younger brother, if parents seem to give him more affection than her, she immediately retaliates against him. In particular, the reaction and revenge of Taeju are appalling each time because mom shows a lot of love for her younger brother.

I'm trying to show my unrelenting affection for Taeju, too. I also talk to Taeju a lot. I explain that Taeju received more love from family when she was young and persuade her that there are many things Taye can't do for himself because he is still young, so his mom and dad help him. Although Taeju is still judges everything by absolute equality in her relationship with her younger brother, when she grows up a little bit further, she will vaguely understand the concept of relative equality.

Taye is now talking a little bit after two years and learning about the concept of possession, so he refuses to take away anything like a toy from his sister. When Taeju pushes, punches, or tries to take away his toys, Taye is aggressive by

Attending an event in the Community Center

grabbing her hair and biting her. Then the house is in a mess, both crying.

The best way to deal with this is to take some time to calm down or time out. And if no one has done anything particularly wrong, I do not side with one and blame the other equally.

Spanking and Prisoning

When the children didn't listen to their parents, and the parents were so tired, my wife usually slapped them on the butt, or I gave them a 10-minute separation in one room. According to the book <Your Child>, published by the American Academy of Child & Adolescent Psychiatry, spanking is not suitable for any reason, and children end up learning violence rather than reflecting on their wrongdoings by being hit in the butt.

The reason I chose to isolate as a punishment is that when my wife was having a hard time with kids, it was necessary to separate the two and allow them time to rest. But Taye cries louder so that he won't be alone in the room, and my wife in the living room or kitchen can't feel at home to hear it. It is also mentioned in <Your Child>, which in turn only confirms that an influential person can punish a weak person. And some kids are usually reluctant to enter the room.

However, since children do not obey their parents just in kind words, another way is to explain to the child that he or she should take time to reflect on themselves in the living room, and to have time for the parents to go into the room instead. Of course, if I don't lock the door, Taye will follow his mom crying to the end of hell.

Good surroundings for children

It is a perfect environment for children to run around, read books, and socialize with people from many countries around the world.

Meadowbrook Park

At the distance of ten minutes from home, there is a big park called Meadowbrook park and a playground made of wood that children like.

Indonesia dance at Community Center

Since the graduate family housing here is a gathering of people from all over the world, community centers often organize their unique events. I watched traditional Indonesian dance performances and got to know a small country in Africa called Liberia.

The church offers a child care service during adult service hours, so you can have comfortable worship and enjoy the joy of being freed from children even then.

Toy-train play in the Urbana library

The Urbana or Champaign libraries offer many of children's favorite books, toys, and family-friendly education programs.

Snow Sleds

There is a hill slightly high next to the housing, and it turns into a snow sled rink in winter. It is better to ride than expected and has a long way down. We put a plastic bag on the floor to a swimming tube, but it doesn't slip well. It is not the ice floor but the snow which has just come, so the friction seems to be substantial.

The sledge of the Orchard Downs hill

One day, there was a snow sled thrown away in the garbage container, so I brought it to repair and ride it. The side is a bit broken, but it looks useful if I can sew it up with a big stapler. It wasn't easy, so I ended up riding it with duct tape. It was working and so fast. I was funny, but the kids were cold and didn't get on much. The winter here was so severe that Taye's face was frozen in 10 minutes.

The snow sled from garbage container

1.5 Culture: People are All Alike

People are all alike

Although American culture is somewhat different from Korea, it is quite similar everywhere people live. Rather than the difference between the U.S. and Korea, here is a quiet college town, not a big city, and people's education and living level are generally good, so people are decent and less frictional. It is the common man's heart that only when one's life is somewhat satisfying and comfortable, one can treat others well. Anyone who goes beyond this is called a good man or a priest.

People here are usually kind, but some bus drivers don't answer back even though I say hello first. The unfriendliness of Champaign DMV which handle car-related registrations and administer driver's license tests is already notorious. As there are many international students, if they want to take a driving test during a semester, they have to wait five hours from dawn to get a chance to take a driving test, but they have no intention of improving the situation and are laughing and talking among themselves.

It is also the truth of the human world that things progress only when those in need must be active first. In particular, the U.S. has an influential culture of individualism that nobody helps unless one actively claims one's rights. Once I went to Urbana Walmart to exchange TV. It was a TCL 32-inch product, which was very cheap compared to Samsung products, as I bought it for about $150. Within 20 days from purchase, however, a line was formed on the screen, making it impossible to use it.

In the United States, exchanges and refunds are relatively easy and ordinary, but the problem is that I do not have the receipt. At that time, I paid with cash because the check card was not issued yet, and I did not consider keeping the receipt because the receipt was so long with other groceries. It was my fault that I failed to keep the receipt, but I admitted that and told an employee to look up the details of the purchase, saying the date and approximate time of the purchase, and the other items we bought together.

An employee at the customer service center said, "I looked it up a few times, and I can't find it," adding, "This cannot be returned." Even though I made it clear that I bought it there, she kept asking if I bought it on the Internet. In the process, there were several times when I didn't understand the words of this black lady, and she shook her head and got the next client with a look of tiredness. If it were a small product, I could have given up, but I couldn't understand why they couldn't find the purchase details when they sold such a big TV and I took a box with a serial number.

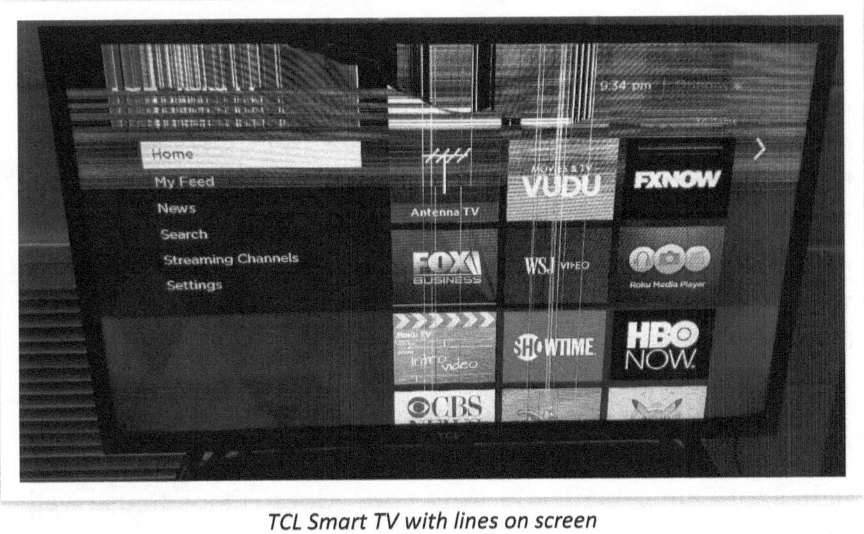

TCL Smart TV with lines on screen

I was angry and felt I shouldn't have to back out of here, so I asked her to call me a manager. The manager came, and after trying many times, he finally found out what I had bought. I got a full refund from the sheepish employee and came home thinking that people are all alike.

In the <Meditations>, Marcus Aurelius said that it is a human duty to love even those who commit wrongdoing. (Book7, 22)

"And, above all, that the man has not harmed you – he has not made your directing mind worse than it was before."

Eye contact and smile with a passerby

If we look at a slightly different American culture, Americans often greet each other with eye contact. Of course, some people don't, but that's what most of the time is. It is partly because it's relatively rural, and people's lives are not tight, but it feels like a kind of American custom. It could have been a habit of checking safety since it is a country where guns are allowed, and there are many crimes.

They often greet each other while jogging in the morning, and even at the mart, they say hello when they are in front of each other. In Korea, it's typical to bow down and show courtesy, but Americans say simple greetings such as "Hi," "Hello" and "Good morning." "Good morning," "Good afternoon" is known as a more formal greeting than "Hi," so it is more appropriate when it comes to relationships that are unfamiliar or require courtesy.

At the ALDI mart, the cashier always asks, "How are you?" before paying the bill, but the answer always seems to be in a tight spot. "Fine, thank you. And you?" doesn't look to use well and usually answers 'good' or 'not bad.' And it is said that it is polite to return the questions, but I am afraid that the words will continue.

It's true that as you get older, you don't have much to laugh. And I used to feel very tired that I had to show a smile on purpose when I met someone even though it wasn't fun. At least in my case, a forced laugh is very unnatural. But there will be no one in the universe who likes frowning faces. I looked up what I was talking about in the <Meditations>. (Book7, 24)

"A deep scowl on the face is contrary to nature, and when it becomes habitual expressiveness begins to die or is even finally extinguished beyond rekindling. Try to attend to this very point, that this is something against reason. In the field of moral behavior, if even the consciousness of doing wrong is lost, what reason is there left for a living?"

Don't leave kids alone, parents always care

Parents would be comfortable and pleasant if kids go outside and play together with friends for a while, but Americans think it's hazardous to play outside without parental care. The U.S. has a lot of roads in front of the house. If kids play in front of the house, they can go to the street as well. Most of our graduate school dorms have quiet roads, but people don't like the situation itself.

Once, Taye wandered out of the house without parents' care. There was a report coming in, and someone came from the apartment office of the university housing. They consulted: never let the children go out alone, and when they played outside, their guardians should always care for them.

Under the Child Welfare Act, it is also illegal for children up to the age of 12 to stay home alone without their parents. There are many things that I can't do at my disposal, even in my own house. It is stricter, especially when it comes to child problems. Parents are obligated to look at a child as a complete person and care until he or she grows up to be an adult.

There is a funny story in the U.S. cartoon, 'The Simpsons.' The main character is Bart, whose mom is annoyed, and she asks Bart to go out and play. While watching Bart play in the playground without his parents, a mother of another child, who played with Bart, called the police and eventually Bart's mom, Marge was arrested.

She said in the court, "When I was young, I used to play outside all day without my mom, then come home at sunset." When she protested that she could not understand the current situation, police immediately arrested Bart's grandmother (Marge's mother) in the audience at the order of the judge.

The scene of Bart's grandmother being arrested

Halloween is a big holiday

Halloween is a prevalent holiday in America. Halloween is said to be the custom of Celtic, but even in Korea, many elementary schools and kindergartens took care of it in the 2000s. Although it is due to the increasing number of children and parents who have experienced the western culture, it will be more likely that the business tactics are encouraging.

A driver's Halloween costume on the bus home

Halloween is October 31st, and it's the custom of giving kids a pre-packaged candy when they go around the house screaming, "Trick or treat!" They often make a Jack-o-lantern out of yellow and big pumpkins and hang it in front of homes.

On the way to school on Halloween, I could see girls wearing makeup on their faces or unique and cute clothes. Look at the Halloween costume of the bus driver. How bold and lovely.

Culture of sharing food at Thanksgiving

Thanksgiving holiday falls to about a week at the end of November, a period during which students take care of their insufficient study and recharge their stamina before the final exam. Without this holiday, it might have been mentally and physically knocked down. Anyway, at this time, it is one culture to share the food and to invite international students to serve the food in American families. In the case of our finance professor, he said: "If you have nothing to do, come to my house and eat together."

I frequently visited David and Ruth's home at Bible study, Friday evening, and sometimes shared the food that we had prepared on a potluck basis. And Thanksgiving is also a day like Chuseok in Korea, so when I put Hanbok on my children, people praised that they are all pretty.

Christmas celebration from a month ago

Christmas is to celebrate the birth of Jesus. For Westerners whose Christian culture is deeply rooted, Christmas is even more special. This year, Christmas Eve is Sunday, so the worship covered the Christmas story (Luke 2:22-35). At 6 p.m., we gathered again to hold an event called Eve Candle Light Service and sang Christmas songs together.

Culture of caring for the disabled & the weak

Disabled people and the elderly can also ride buses in the U.S. Fold the chair and lower the height of the front door to accommodate the wheelchair or stroller in front. It's called 'kneeling,' and there's a sticker called 'kneeling bus' next to the door of the bus.

Stroller in a bus front seat

Part 2. Second Semester (Spring 2018)

The second semester was a little bit better than the first, but it was still hard. If I had learned basic subjects in the first semester, the contents of this semester were complicated because they are the core subjects of financial engineering. It includes 'Derivative theory,' 'Financial risk management,' 'Numerical method,' and 'Stochastic calculus.'

I did my homework faster than before and made more effort at studying for the exam, but it was still not easy to do well. I had a hard time in my busy schedule. I had two team projects, but I did well, and I learned something from others. Overall, this semester's performance is slightly higher than that of the first semester, achieving somewhat above average.

Like the previous semester, I hardly invested my time in studying English. English speaking in the school classes was better than the first semester, but the personal conversation was still tricky because of speed problems and so on. I always feel that speaking is the second important, and the most important thing is to listen and understand correctly. Anyway, just like other universities, some professors are good at teaching, and others are not.

Taeju is now six years old, finishing Kindergarten this semester and becoming the first grader. During the winter break, she only watched her tablet, and her English has improved a lot. She always makes a fuss in English at school or with her friends. Though she cannot say various expressions yet, she is confident. Her English is improving fast as she repeated it over and over again.

Taye also speaks Korean a lot better, so he can express his opinions and understands most of what mom and dad say. However, our apartment building is still noisy. Once he cries, he pulls it up from the bottom of the belly with all his might.

2.1 School: Class Notes with Touch-Pen

LASIK operations and far-sight

I don't feel it when I look at the scenery, but these days, books and smartphone text is blurry and difficult to read. I was worried that I might have a cataract problem, so I went to the McKinley Health Center and asked. The result of the examination was clear that the presbyopia has just come. The doctor advised me to buy a magnifying glass at the mart or the optician. He kindly asked me to try out his reading glasses and taught me how to put down the glasses when reading a book.

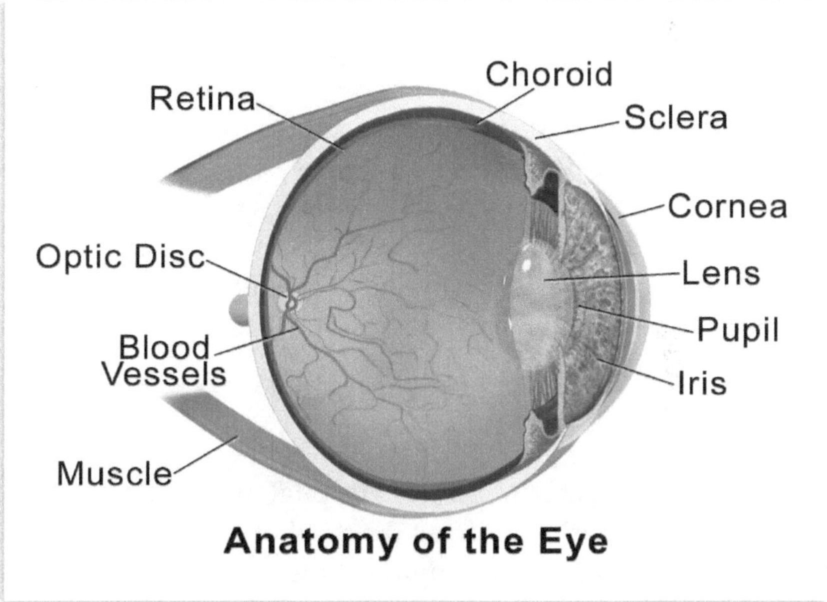

Source: wikipedia.org

I also got presbyopia that people usually have in their mid-40s. Presbyopia happens when the lens of the eye becomes stiff, and the image is not kept clear in the retina, and it is said that this phenomenon is progressing slowly from the 20s.

I had LASIK surgery 20 years ago and have heard that LASIK surgery can cause presbyopia to come quickly. However, LASIK or LASEK is corrective to the cornea and therefore not directly related to presbyopia. However, if you haven't had LASIK surgery, you can help your nearsightedness problems the other way around. In other words, when the nearsighted eyes of youth become dilatory, the focal length will fit, allowing the reader to read books without glasses. Of course, it cannot be permanent, and as presbyopia gets worse, a magnifying glass will be needed as well.

It will be embarrassing for a student, not a professor, to wear magnifying glasses and look down in the classroom, so I looked for ways to overcome it with eye exercises instead of magnifying glasses. Adjusting the thickness of the lens is likely to be possible with eye exercises because it is the muscles around the lens, and the presbyopia comes from weakening the muscles. There are two main ways to exercise: one is to roll your eyeballs up and down, and the other is to lift your forefinger and look at the fingertip while moving it back and forth. With this exercise, I want to live by reading a book without glasses until I'm 80.

Flu shot

The ophthalmologist at McKinley Hospital, who has examined me, recommended that I can get the flu shot on the first floor if I didn't get it. When I was studying at the engineering library, I often heard that someone who would get a flu shot should come down now. My career experience has made me wonder if these people should improve their flu shot inoculation performance. Anyway, I never got hit, so I thought it would be okay to get hit once in my experience. But, there were so many people waiting before me, so I just turned around.

When I came to my house and searched on the Internet, there was a controversy over whether or not to take a flu shot. Some netizens argued the reason of the flu shot as a conspiracy between a pharmaceutical company and a hospital, while another guy, who is presumed to be a doctor, said, "If you don't want to get the flu shot, don't just get hit by you. Do not instigate others with false information." Some people said they felt a bad cold and felt worse after being hit by the flu shot. According to the newspaper, this year's flu shot is slightly underperformed. They usually mix and dilute several flu viruses that are likely to hit that year and give injections. But this year, the hit rate has been reduced, which is said to have had little effect.

For me, as a naturalist who thinks artificial things are bad, I also feel unnecessary taking a flu shot. However, some senior citizens will be able to pass over the flu-related problems with a single flu shot, while others will be able to prevent the flu epidemic by increasing the flu shots inoculation rate among students living in a group.

A professor's advice on life

Neil Pearson is a professor of finance with a head like a monk, who is kind to students. Rumor has it that the amount covered by the class in one semester is equal to the sum of two or three other subjects. Anyway, in the first class, I heard two valuable life tips from him.

First of all, in learning something, reading is useful and vital. In other words, students were advised to keep reading.

Second, living a regular life is a way to increase the chances of success significantly. He also said it is good to keep up with 8 am to 7 pm according to Wall Street's lifestyle.

The importance of reading is the most critical topic in 2018, which I deeply sympathize with, and so is punctual living. However, as a graduate student with a family, there are times I can't control, so the great principle is to finish each subject's assignment within the day and read the text in the evening or on the weekends.

Though slightly different from day to day, 9 am to 6 pm, and 8 pm to 11 pm is my study patterns, including morning and afternoon classes, of course. Last semester, I felt like class hours were taking away my study time, so I had to convert it into part of my study.

Educational capitalism

As I started my new semester, I wrote down my resolutions and thoughts in secret.

> "The registration fee I pay for one semester at the University of Illinois is enormous, so why did I live like that last semester?
>
> First of all, if I think about the most expensive item, tuition, among the registration fee categories, professors are obliged to provide me with proper education and answers, so I have to ask and learn them whenever I have time.
>
> Also, use fitness facilities often to build up your physical strength and concentrate on studying. The fees for McKinley Health Center are already included in the registration fee, so let's make sure to use it when you're not feeling well or needing medical attention."

Analysis of shoulder pain

My injured shoulder at the beginning of last fall semester didn't get much better even after five months. After two months of physical therapy exercise, no significant changes have been made, although it was reassuring to hear from McKinley Health Center that there were no abnormalities in bones or joints. So, I figured I'd have to get to know and deal with it myself.

The shoulder was a very complicated place with more muscles and joints than I thought. So, shoulder pain is said to be a

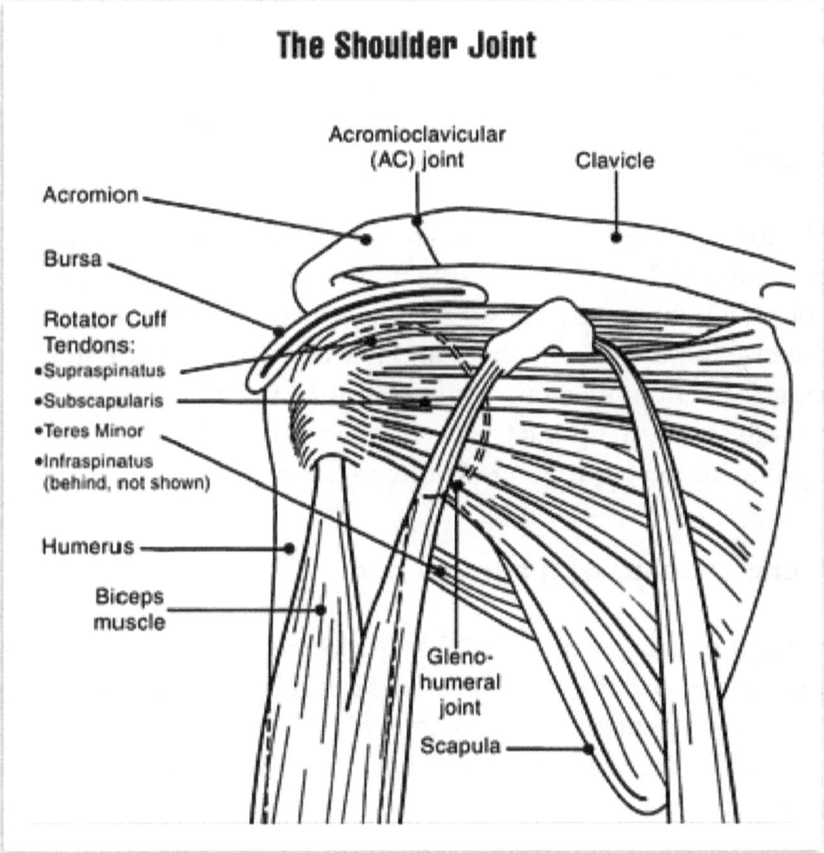

Source: wikipedia.org

common symptom for 3 out of 10 people. The shoulder consists of three bones, four joints, and four rotator cuffs. The three bones are the scapula, clavicle, and humerus, and the four rotated cuffs are the supraspinatus, infraspinatus, teres minor, and subscapularis. The rotator cuff is a tendon attached to the end of the shoulder muscle, which holds the shoulder joints tightly together and enables rotational motion.

However, the rotational cuff tendon is made of hard fibers to hold the shoulder joints stable. Therefore, there is a disadvantage of being easily torn due to lack of flexibility, and recovery is slow when there is a problem as there is less blood flow than soft tissue. I understand that the restoration of my left shoulder is so gradual that there is no significant difference even after five months, and the cause of the pain is thought to be the partial rupture of the supraspinatus rotator cuff and the mass of the surrounding muscles.

The most accurate diagnosis is to take an MRI but given the problems of the rotational cuff and the surrounding muscles, it does not seem to require surgical treatment. In this case, exercise therapy is a method, and it is essential to secure the range of joint movement through stretching before exercising muscle strength. I think the rowing machine, which is equivalent to boat rowing, would be good.

A class memo with a touch pen

My laptop computer is a YOGA 710 15-inch product of Lenovo and has a capacitive touch screen. I can draw pictures or write letters with a touch pen, also known as a stylus pen. Of course, some of the YOGA series have high-priced models with active-type touch pens, but in this case, the pen needs batteries, which makes it more appropriate for me to use passive touch screens.

Most of the notes on class materials are made by touch pens this semester, and the program 'PDF Annotator' is useful. More fundamentally, touchscreen laptops are beneficial. If you keep manipulating things with your keyboard or mouse, your shoulders will get tired quickly, and the touch screen is a good alternative. I don't think laptops that don't have touch screens are going to be my purchase target next time.

Also, the most significant change from college in the '90s seems to be that college students rarely carry paper books these days. There are many free PDF files of textbooks in the U.S., and students usually download them and take notes while looking at them on a tablet or laptop. It's a convenient way because paper books are costly and burdensome. Also, there's not much time to look at them carefully.

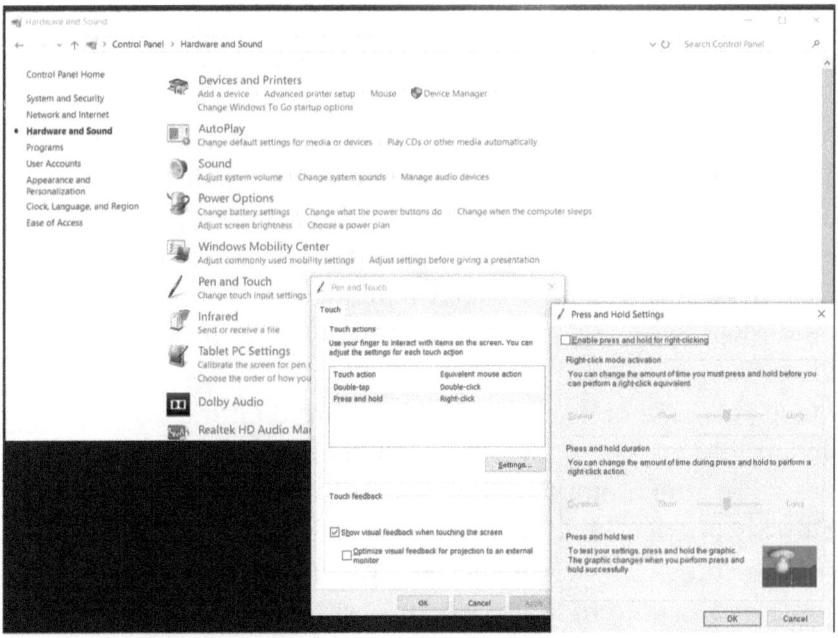

Disable the press & hold recognition with a right mouse click

One thing is, if you take notes with a touch pen, when you tried to write a small letter, you would be perceived as pressing and holding a pen, and you would execute a right click, which resulted in a problem with the context menu. Here's how to disable this feature in Windows 10.

1. On the start menu, type 'control'
2. Select 'Control Panel'
3. Click on 'Hardware and Sound'
4. Then click on 'Pen and Touch'
5. Now you can see the dialog

Steroid ointment and misdiagnosis

I've wanted to scratch my ankle and shin from two or three months ago. I went to the McKinley Health Center, my health helper, and I showed it to the doctor. He asked if I ever wore short pants. After hearing this and that, he said, "I think it's because you jogged the grass wearing shorts. Then I'll prescribe steroid ointment, so try it for two weeks."

Ironically, in well-insured Korea, I was thinking about going to a hospital once a year, but here in the United States, where insurance is weak, there are school health centers nearby, and medical fees are already included in tuition, so I often go there. Of course, students have to pay a little extra charge for the prescribed drugs. Steroid ointment was five dollars.

Maybe because of the side effects of steroid ointment, the doctor told me not to try it for more than two weeks in a row. But, even after a month of rest after applying it, it usually didn't get better. I had to go to the health center again during summer break to consult another doctor, and I got a completely different diagnosis and prescription that fungus seems to be the cause like previous toe eczema. Finally, the second doctor was right, and when I took medicine and applied it, the ticklish thing disappeared that day.

I have seen the following on the online community of Korean residents in the U.S. He said that he wanted to sue the American lawyer who asked to apply for permanent residency, saying that the lawyer lied to him and cheated him out of time. The lawyer didn't even submit the application for permanent residency. One of the most impressive comments was the advice that to avoid fraud in the U.S., one has to have some knowledge of lawyers, doctors, and accountants, and even if commissioned, one has to check everything in person.

All three areas - lawyers, doctors, and accountants - are essential to break away from our daily lives. In my case, it's just a simple misdiagnosis of skin eczema and a doctor is human, but more than that is happening in this world. You should know some of the three fields yourself, so you can live without being fooled by the world.

Visual Studio Memory Issues

Most of the CPUs in today's computers are 64-bit designs. But it is meaningless without software support. It is true of Microsoft Visual Studios, which are programming software. Visual Studios are limited to two gigabytes of available memory when they operate on 32-bit machines. However, there is a way to significantly increase the memory limit by running it as a 64-bit machine.

You need to set two settings: Linker->Advanced->Target Machine, which appears when you right-click a project.

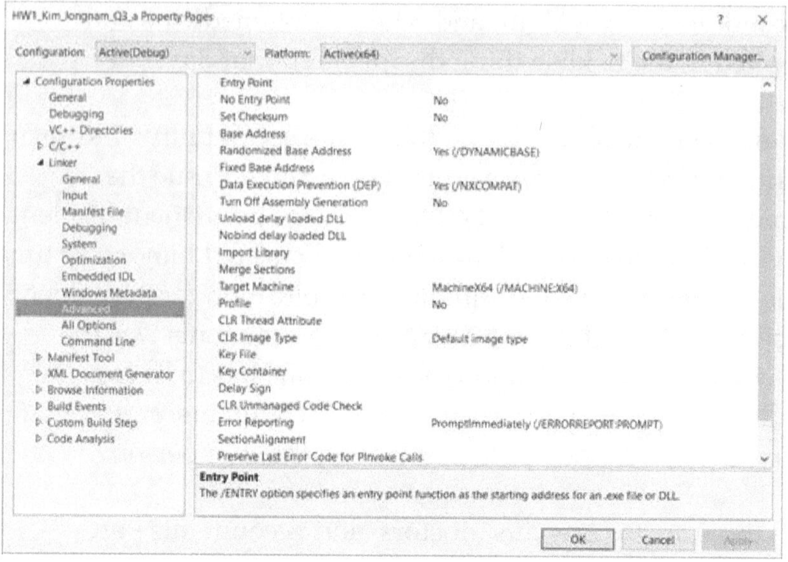

Sets the target machine to 64-bit in project properties

The other item is called Configuration Manager in the Build menu. Change the Active Solution Platform here.

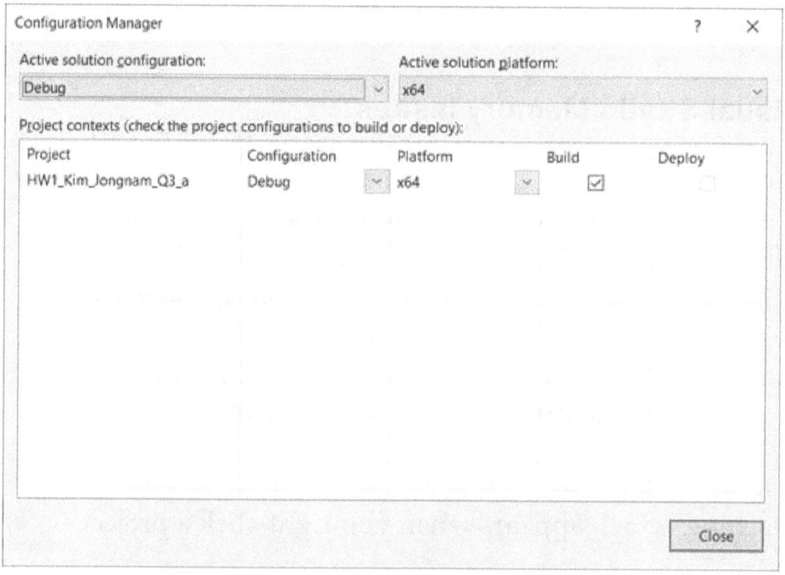

Sets the platform to 64-bit under Build Options

Chicago remote class

Stochastic calculus classes take place every Friday for three hours, once a month in Chicago. It seems to reflect two conditions that the professor's family is in Chicago, and some students are having a practicum class in Chicago on Thursday and Friday. Most of the students in Champaign take classes in existing classrooms on the same day with a remote system.

When I took a remote class, I heard a clear voice from the professor who teaches in Chicago, but the level of concentration in the class has decreased. It seems necessary to use the slide screen more efficiently. For example, if the professor gives a lecture with a red pen on the slide screen, students in remote areas will be much more focused. Even if we don't have to take remote classes, this method can be useful for regular courses because most of the courses these days are conducted with slide materials on screen rather than writing on the blackboard.

Embarrassed in case-study class

In the Financial Derivatives class, there are a total of 14 case studies during the semester, which is often arbitrarily pointed out by the professor to ask for their participation. In other words, a cold call is frequent during case study time.

Today was a case related to Citigroup. In a nutshell, during the 2008 financial crisis, Citigroup announced that it would convert preferred shares into common stocks in consideration of budget needs, and since the conversion ratio was fixed at around 7:3, the change in share prices caused the opportunity for arbitrage trading. To make a profit at this time, preferred stocks had to be 'long' and ordinary shares borrowed and 'short,' but the borrowing cost soared tremendously to nearly 77 percent.

I understood the rough details, but the case study's questions were complicated and specific, and the professor's words were quick. It is not only a problem today, but I thought it was challenging to keep up with the flow of the professor's thinking.

Today, the professor pointed out me and asked about the problem of question number one, but I couldn't get the gist of the content well, and I was nervous about the quick English question so that I couldn't answer at all. "Sorry I don't understand. Would you speak again?" That is all I said to buy time to think again. The correct answer is that even though there are seemingly opportunities for arbitrage profit, it is not much considering the borrowing cost of that time.

Anyway, I listened quietly in class for six months, and today was an embarrassing moment when my English and understanding of the subject were revealed in course. While it is partly due to my nervousness, I first admit that my current English and financial engineering skills are about that level.

And now that I am so embarrassed, I will make it a habit to ask one question in every class. Even if my English is poor and my brain is not smart enough, such an attitude will be much more helpful to me in my life.

Class slides and textbooks

Most of the lectures are done by presenting a slide or a PDF file created by the professors. And three to four textbooks are presented for study. The contents of the slide can be viewed as a synthesis of material from various sources, focusing on what the professor sees as crucial, including the suggested textbooks.

What was always frustrating for students was that the slides the professor made on his own were harder to understand and more time-consuming. I hope we can get a textbook that we call the 'Bible' in the field and focus on its contents. Books that have long been used as textbooks often provide PowerPoint materials for lecturers.

However, as all professors use their slides for class materials, students are often in a hurry to understand the content, and they don't have time to read the textbooks. For example, one class material, which is 20-30 pages long each time, is a condensation of what the professor has studied and agonized for decades, which is profound but not easily understood.

On the other hand, Professor John Hull's book, which is a 'Bible' in the theory of derivatives, is well-written to make it easier to read along. Wouldn't it be worthwhile in itself to have a class that makes the content of the Hull book more than 80 percent understandable? It's never good to make everything complicated.

After all, it is possible to take most graduate classes comfortably only if you first understand the 'Bible' textbook and then enter the course. If you should do it in parallel, you have to struggle with time. 'poor and rich' phenomenon of capitalism appears in the study as well - a person who knows a lot can get a lot more by taking the class. In other words, it only works when you're ready for the course. It's a harsh world for poor people like me.

The last train to Guro and a fish cake

It's been a long time since I've been searching for a cartoon called 'The last train to Guro and a fish cake.' It's a bit of a wild and fun internet cartoon that was serialized in a newspaper. Thirteen years ago, when I was wandering around after graduating from the graduate school of computer science, I ate a line of kimbap for dinner and watched it on the computer a lot.

At that time, I slept during the day and woke up in the afternoon, ate kimbap for dinner at school, and studied English at the engineering library until morning. Even though I scored high on the TOEIC test after three months, I remember that my health was hurt by the changed day and night. After that, I have worked over ten years after I got my first job as a contract worker and settled in my second job.

Now I have my wife and two children, and I have a job, and I'm in the U.S. to study, but I think my mind is similar to the time when I was studying with a piece of kimbap. Just now, lunch has been turned into coffee with boiled eggs and chocolate bars, and the pressure on homework and exams that come out every week is more than ever. Classes are difficult, there are many things to study, assignment due is coming up, and I am not ready for case study tomorrow, so I think I happened to find the cartoon under pressure.

What I know from experience is that the more things I have to do now, the more complicated it is, I have to make things simpler for myself. If I try to solve simple things one by one, I will be able to handle complicated situations with surprising ease.

Level difference

Two case studies of the derivative class were conducted. One is about the TARP Warrants during the 2008 financial crisis, and the other is regarding put options related to the IPO of a small company called Arley. Warrants are almost like call options, so both end up being about an option valuation problem.

It seems that it took me a week to understand the contents and write the report, but the professor put two things together in an hour and 20 minutes. There seems to be a significant gap in level from me. This difference can be analyzed into three factors: basic financial knowledge, mastery through repetition, and English skills. The professor has studied a lot over Finance, and since he has been repeating the same cases for years, he seems to know it even if he closes his eyes. Of course, because he is an American, his English ability is excellent, compared to me.

Most of the students seem to have been busy figuring out what they are doing, and there are only a few students who speak what was in the previous year's report to get points for the participation class. This is the case with students who are comfortable with English, and the rest of them are anxious for an hour because they are afraid to get a cold call.

Today, one of my Chinese classmates, who is weak in English, was struggling to answer questions correctly. It was a relatively easy question, but he felt embarrassed because he lacked preparation and was ineffective in English. Thinking of me in the last class, I felt sympathy for him. I heard that he is excellent in programming.

But the world is not beautiful, so one unfaithful student seized the chance to answer. The answer was straightforward, and he could easily understand and respond to the professor in English. He might score a participation point like a hyena.

I just asked one question about something I do not understand. Without some confidence, it is not easy to ask such basic questions. The professor is kind and does not intend to make students suffer, but the students themselves are stiff-necked for fear that they will not be able to answer.

Anyway, I think this is the most critical class in the Financial Engineering course at the University of Illinois that deals with the nature of financial engineering.

Training 100,000 quants

Four hundred years ago, there was a famous philosopher named Yulgok in Korea. His claim was we should train a hundred thousand soldiers against Japan's invasion. The plan failed to come true due to the opposition of other people, and in the end, Korea was destroyed by Japan's attack disastrously.

I insist on training 100,000 quants. Quant refers to a financial expert who quantitatively solves finance problems based on the knowledge of financial engineering. Korea, which has no resources, has no choice but to build up its human power in the financial market if it wants to become a global leader. And to lead the finance industry, quantitative analysis capabilities based on applied mathematics are essential. Therefore, I claim the necessity of training 100,000 quants as the 21st-century version of Yulgok's claim of 100,000 soldiers.

The most important thing is an excellent education to train the quants. It is never a good education to explain confusedly with complicated math equations. In that sense, I am impressed with the books written by Paul Wilmott. He is, of course, an outstanding mathematician, but on the other hand, he is wary of access to financial engineering, which is too engrossed in mathematics. He says, there is no problem in studying quantitative finance if you know the concept of e, log, Taylor series, mean and variance.

After studying well in the U.S., I want to cultivate good quants in Korea. I will explain quants knowledge clearly with elementary mathematics. This task won't be easy, but it's not impossible. Marcus Aurelius is presenting the way in the book <Meditations>. (Book6, 19)

"Do not imagine that, if something is hard for you to achieve, it is therefore impossible for any man: but rather consider anything that is humanly possible and appropriate to lie within your own reach too."

I'm glad I'm Mr. Kim

It is difficult to pronounce my first name 'Jongnam' for Americans, and its shape is strange because it puts two letters, 'Jong' and 'Nam' together. Indeed, it is not a convenient pronunciation, even for Koreans. That is because all three characters have a consonant in the end. In general, naming is usually hard work. I remember having gone through a lot of trouble searching through the mobile app when I was trying to name my children.

The shocking truth was that Kim Jong-Nam (a half brother of North Korean leader Kim Jong Un), who was assassinated in Malaysia, had the same spelling with me in English. There were only differences in hyphen use.

But I'm glad that my last name 'Kim' is easy to pronounce and remember. It would have been even harder if my last name was complicated. I did not like my last name before, which is too common in Korea, but when I come to America, I think it is beautiful and straightforward to remember. I'm glad I'm Mr. Kim.

Two years at school saves 20 years at work

I happened to find a newspaper interview for a friend of mine who is currently a professor in Korea. It took him three years to write his master's thesis in the U.S., which took a while longer than others. But he was able to finish his Ph.D. program well and became a professor since he was able to read the papers calmly every day. And when he was having a hard time, his advisor's advice that "Two hours in the library saves two months in the lab" was a big help. Rather than just being run into an experiment, it is most important to draw a vivid picture of what to do with the research in advance. Two hours in the library would mean this work.

In the same sense, if the day comes when I give newspaper interviews for my juniors, I would say, "The two years at school saves 20 years at work." It is crucial to draw vivid pictures of what you do at work based on your studies at school. A company is not a place to study. Significant research in one's field should have been done before going to work. And based on that, finding a balance between theory and practice while collaborating with people is the best thing you can do in your career.

Starting a company job with just a college diploma will be the end of one's life while competing against others to keep up with it. The company does not allow individuals time to do the main study. And studying such a main subject while working at a company is also harmful to me in many ways. In a word, it becomes a painful life without any leisure.

I realized this fact after more than five years of working, and while I was at work, I tried to fill in the gaps, but it was almost impossible. That is the biggest reason why I took a leave of absence and came to study in the United States.

Setting up the Newmat (C++ matrix library)

Like general engineering, it is often necessary to perform matrix operations in financial engineering. In a multivariable environment, not a single variable, it is convenient to express in vector form and therefore all require matrix operations. The Newmat is a C++ library for matrix operations, which is public for research purposes.

To create a project in a Visual Studio and to use this package in an instant, you need three settings.

First, set up the Newmat header file directory for the project compilation.

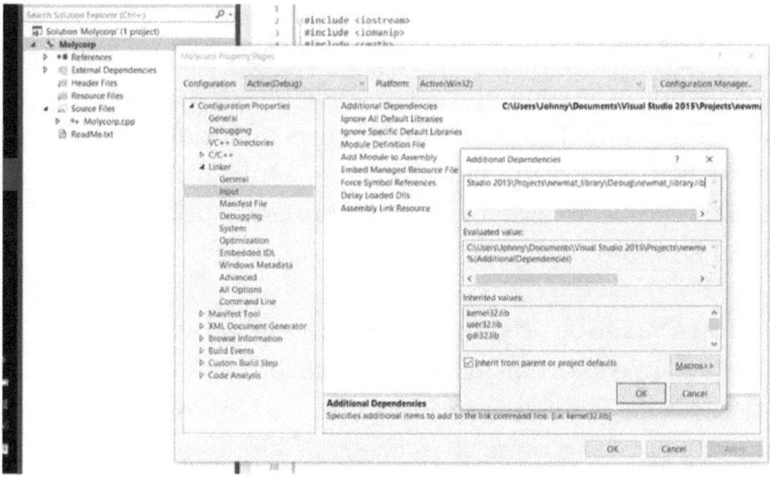

Header file directory settings

Second, for project linking, set up a directory with various obj files.

Finally, set up the dynamic library 'newmat_library.lib.' If you do not have the directory path, you must accompany the path.

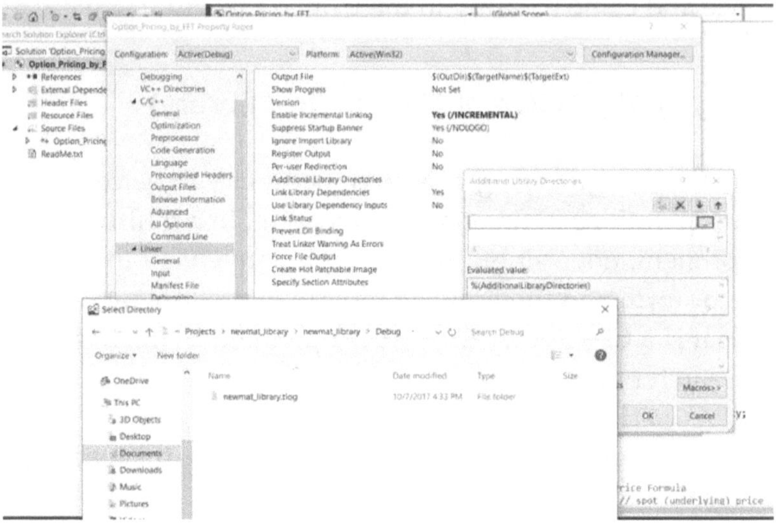

Dynamic library path settings

Microsoft cloud service, OneDrive

As I use the Windows operating system, Microsoft's 'One Drive' is more convenient than 'Google Drive' as a cloud service. I'm using it to synchronize class materials with. Its purpose is to back it up, but it is also useful because class materials can be accessed on smartphones. A ubiquitous study became possible.

A typical OneDrive account is a free five-gigabyte account, which is a little short of a cloud service, but it is possible to use 2,000 gigabytes, which is almost unlimited by using your university email account.

Chicago Class & Seminar

I had a class and a seminar in Chicago, so I took a group bus at 6 a.m. for a day. A quant seminar was held with lunch at 12 - 2 p.m. after receiving a stochastic calculus class.

Busy morning of Chicago

Under the theme, "How I became a quant?" hosted by the International Association for Quantitative Finance (IAQF), we could hear from five-panel members and ask questions. The University of Illinois Financial Engineering program sponsored this Chicago seminar. Among the panels was CTC head quant Dr. Sobczak, whom I saw last year on the Chicago field trip.

Case-study embarrassment ver.2

It was better than the last time I couldn't answer at all, but it didn't go smoothly. There was even a nervous reply to the 2013 CDS skew situation. My answer was unsatisfactory again this time, but if I did well one thing, I didn't avoid it and went to the discussion class, and I talked about it slowly and clearly so that other people could understand it.

Because the contents of the case are complicated, most of them only submit reports, and almost half of the students fail to attend classes to avoid cold calls these days. Besides, it is often difficult to understand what other students talk. They have a conversation only with the professor and speak in a small voice quickly.

Financial Engineering and my aptitude

Having studied financial engineering for a while, it's only now that I can see what a financial engineer is like. Financial engineering is basically like solving optimization problems. It is the job of a financial engineer to think about how to maximize profits by using the tools available.

To put it more bluntly, it seems like the essence of financial engineering to argue, calculate, and kick to make even more money. In this regard, I sometimes wonder if it is the right major for a person like me who doesn't like to calculate if it's not a big problem.

I've had no taste in money since I was a child. I wasn't interested in judging what was beneficial, and even I thought that such a person was too small to do big things. Instead, like the main characters of the <Three Kingdoms> the world's rationales - sometimes seeking, betraying, loving, and breaking up - were more interested. It's ironic that I'm studying to be a financial engineer. I don't know which way to go.

Difference between Finance and Physics

There are too many models in Finance. I'm in a state of confusion. In a joke, a professor once said that Physics explains 97 phenomena under three laws, while Finance tries to explain three things by 97 different models and even that doesn't work.

Those who have ever written an academic paper may feel it, but there are too many useless models in the desire to write a new article by slightly modifying, improving, and developing the existing one. The funny thing is, even the people who make such complex models use simple models when they need a model.

So, I'm not going to make a new finance model. Like the philosophy contained in the Unix pipeline, it is more beautiful to combine the simple things that are already there to create the big, great things.

Urbana–Champaign squirrels

Urbana-Champaign area has many squirrels everywhere. Squirrels in the school quad are especially familiar to humans because people feed them often. Initially, there were squirrels here, but in fact, it was the result of the university president's policy, which is introduced in 1901 to be emotionally helpful for students. Details of that time were also recorded in the University of Illinois Archives.

The squirrel hanging upside down so naturally

2.2 English: Speaking to Oneself

Taeju starts speaking English in 6 months

After watching 12 hours of English cartoons a day on YouTube during two to three weeks of the winter break, it feels like Taeju's English skill has improved. There are three things she says most now: "What are you doing?" "It's mine." and "This is broken."

Although her grammar is often incorrect and mainly based on simple expressions, it is important to tell people with confidence, and pronunciation is also the same as real native because she imitates what she heard. And the most significant advantage of Taeju in learning English is that she is always saying something. Whether the other person listens or not, Taeju keeps talking. When she plays with friends, she speaks English the most even though she is the worst among them.

Speaking to oneself

There is an English book in Korean that my wife praised, <Speaking to myself>. I couldn't buy it at Kyobo bookstore because it was out of stock, but its rough outline is that we will be able to train ourselves throughout the day by murmuring everyday speaking expressions from waking up in the morning to going to bed at night. The phrase "My speaking partner is just myself." strongly comes to me.

1. Imagine your idea

2. Open your mouth

3. Don't stop speaking

On the other hand, there is also a person named Robby, who found enlightenment and established a company after focusing on fluent English. He strongly recommends speaking with oneself in English as an excellent way to chat. He came from Latvia, Eastern Europe, to go abroad for a job in Ireland, and worked hard for five years to speak English fluently. He read English novel books, studied advanced grammar books in depth, and received praise from his colleagues.

After so many years, he saw himself with little improvement in English speaking fluency, and what he realized one day is the simple truth that to be good at speaking, practicing a lot of speaking is the only way to do well. What he lacked was speaking fluency, but what he usually did was reading and writing practice, and he never really had enough time to practice speaking.

> And there's no better way – **as a matter of fact**, it's the ONLY way! – of improving your spoken English than engaging in heavy spoken English practicing.
>
> I've been receiving a lot of questions in relation to this topic.
>
> I mean – specifically about PRACTICING spoken English.
>
> - What's the best way of doing it?
> - What to do when there's no-one else available to practice with?
> - And what to do when I don't know what to talk about?
>
> Every time I respond to these type of questions, I use **pretty much the same** answer because **I know for a fact** it WORKS:
>
> > If you've got no-one else to chat with, you can do it all by yourself – just narrate your thoughts and if you don't know what to talk about, the best topic is to describe what you've been doing during the day and what your plans are for the following day. And in case you're skeptical about this approach – read this article to find out why speaking with yourself isn't so dissimilar to speaking with other people!

Robby's blog suggests speaking with oneself

He studied while driving a forklift in a factory warehouse, learning words at first, then memorizing sentences later, and finally practicing speaking English with himself.

He explains that training to talk to himself in English is useful for thinking in English and is not much different from speaking with others. You don't have to shout for fear that others won't recognize your speaking. It's enough to mutter with a little sound.

To add my thoughts, reading, listening, speaking, and writing is basic ways of thinking in and out of English, but of course, they influence each other. Therefore, to do well in one area, one must practice that area a lot. And active practice like reading out loud, shadowing, or predicting the next one is much more effective.

Wife's study of Spanish

My wife seems to have a goal in American life to master both English and Spanish. More specifically, she said she wants to live in Spain for several years. And she sings along Spanish songs like a trot, so it even haunts my ears. The singing styles all sound alike. She insists that English speaking comes out better on a day when she has studied Spanish.

She also does so-called 'Morning Ritual' every morning, that she has time to memorize all the good paragraphs from newspapers and books. It seems that it takes at least two hours to finish both Spanish and English. Sometimes she memorizes and goes back to sleep because she's tired.

The population of Spanish is substantial in the United States. Spanish-speaking people are called Hispanics and account for nearly 20 percent of the country's total population of 330 million. It is much more than black Americans of 13 percent. Historically, several southwestern states, including Texas, New Mexico, Arizona, and California, and Florida were Spanish lands. The Hispanic population in the U.S. continues to grow, and because of the Catholic culture that has many children, the number of Hispanics in the U.S. is soaring.

In the phone ARS, you can easily hear the message "Press No. 2" if you want to speak Espanyol, and the cable channel is also available in Spanish. Some say that it is difficult to do business in the U.S. without knowing Spanish.

The Spanish language is more than 80 percent similar to Portuguese so that they can communicate with each other to some extent. Even Italian or French is more than 70 percent identical to Spanish, so simple conversations with each other are no problem. The so-called European trilingualism does not seem to be as tricky as Koreans think.

2.3 Life: Where is Spring?

Wife's driving test

U.S. driver's license is quite challenging to pass the road test. My wife has also failed the road test twice in a row. I have to take Taye, a 3-year-old son, for the exam, so she went to the DMV at the beginning of my semester to take the test. I think she'll have to practice a little more and take the third test because she can take the test up to three times with the $30 she paid.

While it is difficult to pass the test because of communication with examiners in English, the U.S. driving test is tricky. It's even not easy for a person to drive a lot in Korea because examiners are checking to make sure that they start after waiting 2-3 seconds for a stop sign, or that they have to turn their heads when changing lanes. It's a point loss if you go too slowly. Furthermore, my wife had only a license and rarely drove in Korea.

What's unique is that those who pass the written test have a driving permit. In other words, only if you pass the writing test, you can drive a car for a year. Driving licenses and driving permits are distinct. The driver who has a driving permit must ride it with the driver who has a driving license, and if an accident occurs, it can be handled with the license owner's insurance. In the case of Progressive auto insurance, the driver was required to be entered separately, whether it was a license or a permit. Adding my wife as a permit did not incur any additional costs.

For your information, F-2 visa holders, including spouses, should be able to spare two weeks more than F-1. If F-2 is to be tested for the first time, qualification will not be done directly from the DMV and confirmation letters should come home from other cities where the headquarters are located. It takes a week or two, and you have to take it and go back to the DMV to take the test.

Defrosting the windshield

When you try to drive in the morning of winter, you can't drive at all because of the dense frost of the windshield. I searched Google because I thought it would take at least 20 minutes if I wait for the frost to melt. The answer is to turn the air conditioner, not the heater, on to the windshield and use washer fluid together.

The reason for the frost is the temperature difference between the inside and outside of the car, so it is said to melt the frost only when the temperature difference is reduced through air conditioning. Because washer fluid has a low freezing point, spraying the washer fluid will also melt the frost. Surprisingly enough, I was able to start three minutes after I did this way. Thanks to that, I'm using a lot of washer fluid this winter, but I bought a gallon at Walmart, so there's no big problem. The price is also about $1.5, which is cheap.

Cemetery in the middle of the city

I've been passing by the cemetery every morning. My heart is pious. Its name is Mount Hope. True hope is not found in the soulless words of the living but on the silent grave of the dead.

Urbana–Champaign cemetery, Mount Hope

Marcus Aurelius probably wrote the book <Meditations> in his old age, because there is a great deal of speaking about death. He was terrified of death, and so he seemed to keep suggesting to himself that death was nothing but natural. (Book4, 48)

"You should always look on human life as short and cheap. Yesterday sperm: tomorrow a mummy or ashes. So one should pass through this tiny fragment of time in tune with nature, and leave it gladly, as an olive might fall when ripe, blessing the earth which bore it and grateful to the tree which gave it growth."

Video call with parents in Korea every week

I tried to supplement the microphone separately because smartphone mike seems to have weak performance, but I can't use it when the kids are playing with it like a toy. I couldn't help but return to Amazon. It's better to make phone calls than not to contact, or to see them in person than to call them.

The cold spell continued in February

Many days are coming in February when the temperature drops below minus 10 degrees Celsius. I went to the car for the church on Sunday morning, and the whole car was covered in ice. No matter how much I start it up and wait with washer fluid, the windshield froze thick enough to show no sign of melting. In this case, lowering the temperature difference by turning on the air conditioner does not seem to mean much.

Thickly frozen windshield

I wish the windshield had some heat. Or wouldn't it melt a little faster if I heated it in with a hair dryer that I could put into the cigar jack? I have to go to the gym Monday morning to work out, and I'm afraid it might freeze hard again. That is why people here seem to prefer a house with an indoor garage.

Winter monsoon rain

It rained like crazy yesterday and today. There is news that it will continue to rain this week. Side-to-side blows characterize Illinois raindrops due to strong winds. The umbrella covers only the upper body, but the bottom is soaked to the skin, as it strikes from the side at an angle of 45 to 30 degrees instead of perpendicular to the ground. It's even hard to hold onto an umbrella in the wind. So somehow, American students here are bold enough to wear a hoodie in the rain. Even now, the sound of rain is still heard without mercy.

Weekends are harder

I believe it's the weekend's role to relax and take time to recharge for next week. But somehow the weekend is unbearable than weekdays. First of all, I have a lot of homework to submit at the beginning of the week, so if I don't nearly finish it on the weekend, I'll have a hard time next week. Plus, since Taeju does not go to school on Saturday and Sunday and stays at home all day, she has a tit-for-tat fight with her younger brother Taye and mother all day long. I can't feel at home when my wife complains about her tiredness.

Maybe it's getting warmer these days, so if the next house or lower house seems to be going somewhere on the weekend, the wife will complain more. However, it is not known whether they went to the mall or went to the mart, and each person is in a different situation. All I have to do is go to the mart together over the weekend. The position of a graduate student with a lot to study and a relatively idle visiting researcher cannot be the same. And if someone hasn't studied hard financial engineering once, I'd like to shout, "Stop talking like that."

Nowadays, there are many times when we don't go to church on Sunday morning to do my homework and prepare for the exam, but that doesn't make my studies efficient on Sundays. So, I feel depressed on weekends these days.

Spring break

I'm planning to go to the nearby Kickapoo state recreational area on this spring break. Kickapoo is the name of the native American tribe and originally lived near the Great Lakes of Michigan and Wisconsin before moving south to Illinois. I've heard a lot of compliments from many people, but when I looked into the website to visit there, it's hard to make a reservation.

Reservations are made on a separate site called 'Reserve America,' and the terms of camping are confusing. As far as I understand, the booking will be made from May, and currently, it says 'walk-up.' When I googled it, I found walk-up means first-come-first-served, and it usually goes when off-season, not during peak season. There is also the term 'walk-in,' which refers to a camping site where you have to get out of your car and walk in the forest.

We're going to pack some lunch and have a picnic on Saturday, but it's for the first time, so I'm afraid we're going to

A lake in the Kickapoo state park

make a lot of trial and error. Like the financial markets, if you can't predict the future, you're in a precarious and uncertain situation. Some may enjoy such uncertainty, but that is only possible when I backpack through my 20s. Now, my family needs to hedge risks while predicting as much as possible because American life itself is an adventure to my family.

A monk's theory of human relations

While studying the Numerical Methods in the library, suddenly words about human relations came to mind in a book by Rev. Hyemin, <Things can be seen when you stop>.

I don't know why this article came to mind all of a sudden. Maybe it's because Hyemin also studied in the U.S. for a long time?

There are three things that Buddhist monk Hyemin realized when he was in his 30s.

> First, someone else is never as interested in me as I think.
>
> Second, I realize that everyone in the world doesn't have to like me.
>
> Third, all the things that I do for others, in the end, are for me.

So, the bottom line is, don't be so conscious of other people and live doing what you want to do. It's a simple but fantastic realization. I think this idea is an excellent insight that has the essence of life through words.

Three tips for running posture: CHP

I'm running in the school gym two or three times a week, and I remember the 'CHP' position I read in the book <Marathon> about the right posture. The author said to memorize it as CHP, or California Highway Patrol. The author Jeff Galloway seems to live in California.

Anyway, if you raise your chest and run forward with the hip, you feel that your posture improves, you don't get tired quickly, and your speed is much faster. However, I cannot yet feel the force of using my ankle as a lever. Anyway, this is a good posture not only for running but also for regular walking.

In the same sense, it is crucial for the chest to lead a body like a car headlight. That is what a woman from San Francisco who I met on a trip to Hawaii told me.

1. C (Chest Up)

Raise your chest. Take a deep breath, and then hold your forward position when you breathe. You think you tied it to your chest by tying a rope to a pulley. The other side of the pulley is tied up in a three-story building, a section away. When you start running, raise your chest and push it forward. Keep your chest ahead. Don't bend forward, lift up your chest, and stick it out front. That increases your lung capacity. Don't change your shoulders or arms. You can get a better posture and lung efficiency with just your chest.

2. H (Hips Forward)

Stretch your chest forward, and the hips automatically move forward. Put your chest up before you run, put your hands on your hips, and push forward. Shoulders, heads, hips, and legs will all be in line. In this position, maximum force is transmitted to the legs. When the hips come forward, you feel that calf muscles are used, and you can hardly feel the use of your thighs. When the hips come forward, you feel a lighter step and can run more quietly.

3. P (Push Off)

Push your feet hard. Stretching your chest and hips forward will place your ankles in position, allowing you to effectively use the force you push from your feet even with the small force of your calf muscles.

Most runners run a little backward, so they have to overcome gravity at every step. The point of wear on the heel of the shoe tells that. It's good to touch the ground with your heel, but you shouldn't put your weight on your heel. It's not good for your knees. The knee bones are attached tightly to your knees so that you may grind cartilage into your bones. When the ankle does its job, the tension on this knee is considerably reduced.

Naturally, if you are a person whose back spindle touches the ground first, don't try to move your weight to the front of your feet suddenly. After contacting the ground, shift your weight to the center of your foot, and use the lever on your ankle. Finally, push off the field with your toes. Gradually turn the running into an ankle reflex. Then you'll feel like you're floating instead of banging on the ground.

Snow in late March

It snowed quite a bit in spring break. I heard that there was more snow in the east, so I wonder whether this is spring. The same is true of Korea, so spring and fall are getting shorter, and summer and winter are getting longer. Simple is beautiful, so I guess God is trying to simplify the season into two.

In late March, it snows in large flakes

Rather than the stark spring here, where there is no leaf, once snow accumulates, it seems that my heart feels warm. However, there was as much snow as in January to say it was snowing in the spring and blizzard is blowing sideways. Maybe it's the last chance to ride a snow sled on the hill behind Orchard Downs.

Where is spring?

It snowed in April. I thought March would be the last snow, but it snowed a lot today. I heard it's minus 6 degrees tomorrow morning, so I can't believe it is April weather. Should I be glad I still have a chance to sled down the hill? Anyway, it's spring semester, but there's no spring.

I had a Jim Beam bourbon on ice over dinner. A four-year-old, 40-degree white label is typical. The price is just under $15. Jim Beam is an American national whiskey comparable to Soju in

Korea. It was made by Beam families in Kentucky and became one of the best-selling brands of bourbon in the world.

American's national bourbon whiskey, Jim Beam

Tomorrow Monday, the stochastic calculus test and Tuesday's case study are just around the corner. When will spring come to me?

There is a saying in the Epictetus' collection of famous words. Epictetus' writings had a significant impact on Marcus Aurelius' <Meditations>.

"True teaching is one that allows you to learn to be satisfied with everything that happens to you. How can that be possible? It's because the God of all affairs has set it so. God has laid all things that way so that there is winter in summer, famine in a good harvest, evil in good, so that everything is matched up against each other, and harmonized as a whole."

Wife's love of rap

My wife sang Spanish songs for a while, but nowadays she's so into 'Eminem' that she sings the rap every morning. With the praise that Eminem's rap and voice are so superior that no one can keep up with it. I was curious, so I searched a little on the net. The title of "White rapper who becomes legend in black music" comes as a strong impression. Sure enough, since he had a woefully unhappy childhood and had a rap battle for a living, he was determined to win the prize by beating the opponent even if he didn't win. In other words, he's prepared to make a decision that he's either killed or stood tall in the world by rap music.

Once I hear my wife sing a rap, she's out of breath. She didn't breathe in time. No matter how continuous the rap seems, it seems that we can only continue if we can set a short break in the middle. I guess rap isn't just about everyone, but it's a profound genre. And most of all, I have a hard time studying while she's rapping every morning, so I get mad.

Radio worship service

FM 89.3 Mhz, Illinois Champaign region. I am listening to Christian radio when I go to the gym in the morning and go to the mart by car on the weekend. The word 'resurrection' came out a lot today because it's Easter week.

Sudden summer weather from May

The weather has suddenly changed since May. A little green color is about to be seen on the branches that had no sign of sprouting leaves. The cold ground of the earth is now slightly warmer. After finishing the final exam with studying nearly for about ten days, the summer break that I had been waiting for comes. Wait for me, United States West.

2.4 Parenting: Co-Parenting with YouTube

Parenting goal

Studying in the U.S., we are the first to live with a four-member family wholly, and my wife and I also started parenting nearly for the first time. It is essential for Taeju to get into the habit of eating a full meal in about 20 minutes, which is not too long. Taye will practice his toilet training until the end of the year when he turns three years old.

Valentine's Day cards

A few days ago, there was a home message from Taeju's school asking for a card to be distributed to friends on Valentine's Day. Although it was not mandatory, other friends seemed to do, so we rushed to find a card form on the Internet and filled out each name and phrase. And my wife painted it with colored pencils. The cards for the four teachers also added a little bit of effort to make a difference between the wording and the cover.

On that evening, I asked Taeju if she had given out the cards, and she answered, "I gave it," and she was busy eating candy and chocolate from her friends. I was worried because Taeju had a fever from the previous day and had a headache.

A few days later, her mom happened to see the Taeju's backpack and found out the card was still there. My wife and I took the time to make a card together, but it was absurd that Taeju didn't give it to them. And I thought we should not let her go of lying. Even if it were a little late, it would be a waste to throw it away, and I sent a message to the homeroom teacher that Taeju would bring it back to school next week.

"Dear Mrs. Puffer,

I am Taeju's dad. We made Valentine's day cards together for friends and teachers. I thought Taeju gave out them to others that day. But, today morning, Taeju's mom found the cards remained in her backpack. Taeju says it was not pretty so she did not give. I think my daughter is studying well in the King school with your effort, but still shy because of English communication and so on. If you don't mind, I'd like to send it again next week. We have already made them, and it's too bad to throw away. Thank you."

Focus on tablets and smartphones

Children usually can't stand still for a second and either bother their parents or beg for help. At least our children do. There are some differences in the way parents teach them, but I think it's their inborn property. When such children watch YouTube videos on their tablets or smartphones, they can sit still for hours. In the case of Taeju, while she watches a YouTube on the tablet, she runs to the bathroom as if she doesn't even have time to go to the bathroom.

It's a crazy concentration. I'm terrified of smartphones. If humankind collapses in the future, it could be because of smartphones, not because of diseases or drugs. The loss of life and spirit due to smartphone addiction is believed to be the cause of the eventual destruction of human beings. In the future, people don't want to meet people, and they're tired of raising children, and watching the smartphone is the greatest comfort. To prevent the collapse of humanity, Apple and Samsung will have to establish a research institute for smartphone addiction therapy and should become social enterprises.

Reading children's Bible

I got a children's Bible from the church to read it to the children, but I am reading it myself. There will be many people in the world who dream of reading the entire Bible once. Regardless of religion, the Bible is said to be the bestseller of humanity, and that such greed is natural.

I have also given up on several occasions while reading the Korean Bible. There are countless stories about who gave birth to whom. It is also problematic that too many Middle Eastern names come out that we cannot understand, and the tone itself is so old that it is unnatural and incomprehensible.

By comparison, the NIV or NIrV versions of the English Bible are entirely natural and are understood by themselves when read. Notably, the children's Bible that I am reading is straightforward, and the story is with the picture, so I have already seen it all.

I happened to read this child's Bible to Taeju in the evening, and the reaction was good, listening quietly and asking questions from time to time. However, she keeps insisting on pronouncing Jesus as [Jises]; I think she learned to pronounce 's' sound at school. Anyway, the important thing is, before we came to the U.S., she hated reading English books in Korea, asking me to read them in Korean, but after attending American school, she seems to have changed a lot. I think it would be 50 times better for a father to read an English book than to give a tablet in terms of child sentiment or education.

Co-parenting with YouTube

My wife says she probably wouldn't have endured American life without the Samsung tablet. Because Taeju tends to stir-fry her parents except for watching a tablet, and Taye stays with his mother all day, it means that my wife has no time to breathe if they don't have time to watch the tablet.

Since Taeju watched English cartoon programs on the tablet during winter break all day long, English has improved a lot. It is a positive effect of YouTube, and the educational information children get from YouTube is also substantial. There is a common-sense scientific program where comedians come out and explain it interestingly, and Taeju often asks for white blood cells and red blood cells when she sees the program.

I don't know exactly if it's tablet co-parenting or YouTube co-parenting, but it's a world where kids are learning a lot from videos. In other sense, their parents need to be educated and prepared enough to talk with such kids.

Taye, second warning of playing on the road

It seems like a neighbor reported to the housing office that Taye kept going to the driveway. I heard he complained that he was nervous and he couldn't live comfortably.

Taye is now two and a half years old, no matter how much we talk, he doesn't listen to parents. He gets the hang of it, but it's a time that he wants to do anything the other way around. Thanks to that, my wife and I were called in for a consultation at the housing office. I explained to Whitney, the housing coordinator, that our couple is taking this situation seriously and that we will pay more attention in the future. And that day, we wore Taye with child harness, which we had ordered from Walmart in advance, to show our determination.

Taye, who wears a child harness and walks the Urbana market

Taye didn't want to wear it at first, but he adjusted to it right away. People laughed, making sure to say "Good idea" one by one when they saw him on a nearby walk or a trip. Many people walk with dogs tied up in leash, and Taye is like a puppy moving forward, so I feel like I have a dog.

School lunch with Taeju

At King School in Taeju, there is a day when parents can come to school and have lunch together. We visited with Taye because we wanted to participate in school events as much as possible. I think it was considerate to eat outside with their parents on purpose, but the sun was too hot on this day. And there were fewer parents present than expected.

Having lunch together at King school

Each class got some food at a restaurant and ate together at an outdoor table. After eating, teachers strictly controlled it so that students could play in outdoor playgrounds and enter each classroom again. Black people were the majority of the students, and sometimes, white or Asian children were seen. Asians are the children living in Orchard Downs, where their parents are attending the University of Illinois.

Taeju and her friend Pfizer are playing after lunch

It seems very desirable and good to hang out with so many different races and groups since childhood. But I'm worried about the picky eating habit of Taeju. She's only trying to eat the crumbs of cookies, not many hamburgers she had received today. Taye, who has a particular stock of soup, only drinks milk today. And the size of the head has already overtaken his older sister.

Taeju will be in first grade

Promotion ceremony in King school

Taeju had a promotion ceremony before the summer break at the end of May. After the summer break, she will be in first grade from the fall semester. What was a little bit unique at the promotion ceremony was that each homeroom teacher appeared in front of students and gave them a listing, naming each of the children in his or her class. Taeju received the Artist Award and the Perfect Attendance Award. Taeju usually likes to draw, so I think Mrs. Puffer made the artist award for her. And many children are less likely to receive a perfect attendance award than I thought.

Car-loving Taye

These days, when Taeju goes out to take the school bus at 7:30 in the morning, Taye accompanies her sister and sees the school bus, sees her off, and goes to the MTD bus stop nearby.

Yesterday, a bus driver asked Taye to sit on the driver's seat and try to drive. Taye's love of the car and the love of the bus is so great. I remember that I liked cars when I was young, but not that much.

School bus 44

Feeding children

The most challenging thing for parents is to feed their children. The same is true of parents whose children are of a similar age on the Internet. Leaving it alone may be one way to do it, but parents often fail to do so because they fear that their child will become malnourished at a time of growing up.

Taeju's 3-day suspension at the Kids Club

Mrs. Sarah, the head of the Kids Club, is said to have lost some chocolate for the event. It turned out that Taeju ate half of them without permission. When Mrs. Sarah asked who took the chocolate to raise a hand, she was angry because Taeju didn't turn herself in. Taeju was punished for being at home and not being able to go to the Kids Club for three days.

Taeju admitted her mistake and reflected on it a little bit but showed a sense of coolness that she'd better not go to the Kids Club.

When I was young, I also remember eating delicious food out of curiosity and lied not to be scolded for it. Although this case was Taeju's faults, the adults also need to be careful to prevent such a situation from happening. And I think it's appropriate to give some punishment and make sure that it doesn't happen again if a fault has already occurred.

Anyway, I'm very grateful to the after-school program at Orchard Downs. It coaches children almost free of charge for two hours a weekday afternoon. And Mrs. Sarah loves children and especially can't resist when Taye asks for candy.

2.5 Culture: Volunteer Society

Volunteer society

American society is the epitome of capitalism, but on the other hand, much is being done by volunteers. It is none other than the culture of participation. When community events are held in an apartment, they always recruit volunteers. Most things are handled by volunteers every week except the preacher in the church system. Someone monitors CCTV, and somebody takes the role of turning over the sermon slides. Some control sound equipment, and some serve in Childcare.

As volunteers are emphasized and encouraged at the social level, it is also economically efficient. And for participants, it will undoubtedly be an experience that can be put into a resume, and there will be learning while working. Regardless of other things, the culture of individual participation as a member of society itself seems to be desirable.

Two old ladies who were close to my wife at Savoy Church

School bus culture

The school bus number that Taeju rides when she goes to King School is 44. School buses in the U.S. are run by the school district in batches and schools use the service, so all school buses have the same shape and just numbered.

School buses are treated specially by traffic regulations, so regular drivers must be cautious. When a school bus opens a stop sign next to the bus to pick up or get off the children, all cars that come and go either way must stop. If this is violated, substantial sanctions are imposed.

Maybe because the bus is yellow and impressive, eighty percent of Taye's head is full of school buses. The most commonly used words for Taye are 'school bus' and 'no.'

Busking

The most enviable and wanted to do in Europe or the United States is playing the guitar and singing on the streets. It is called busking. Of course, it would be better if I were a good musician enough to get enough tips. I want to go on a busking trip to Europe together before the children grow up. Singing while playing the guitar in front of people is a lot different from doing it alone at home. Much more training is needed, and the ability to cope with a variety of unexpected situations is necessary.

Playing guitar and singing at home is similar to studying financial engineering in textbooks and busking in front of people can be likened to working as a quant in Chicago's finance street. Only when you have the flexibility and training to deal with various situations, you can call yourself a real busker, a real financial engineer.

To do busking, I think I need to prepare at least ten songs for the repertoire. And I hope to have a pop song in English that people around the world can understand. After selecting a song, I need guitar practice and singing practice. And I should also think about the equipment for busking, such as a small amplifier. It will be less fun if I do it alone and it will be a good trip for my family as well. Since there is a problem with the children's school, the travel period should be less than two months in the summer.

A jogging-loving country

Many people are jogging in the United States. Some run in the rain and others run in the cold. People of all ages and genders go jogging a lot. The best exercise at no cost is jogging. Running treadmills indoors and running on the street is different in the quality of sweat.

A culture of no concern to others

I saw a yellow-haired Western girl eating on the bus this morning. If I were her and ate my lunch box on the bus, I would be sick from eating.

A few days ago, on a rainy day, three students were walking at school, two men with umbrellas and a woman without an umbrella were walking away from the rain. It was a situation no one would put on, but the girl looked as if nothing had happened to her. But in Korea, men would be blamed for being tactless and lack of manners.

I don't know their surrounding situation exactly, but Americans don't be conscious of others or blame others for such a thing. This aspect seems more comfortable to live in.

There are times when people felt uncomfortable because they did things they didn't have to do only to avoid criticism.

A society that recommends sweets

Americans love sweets. At any event at the Orchard Down Community Center, children are always fed up with snacks such as candy and chocolate. The culture of giving candy and chocolate as gifts on Valentine's Day is to the same effect.

And Taeju does Kids Club in the afternoon at the community center, and I'm crazy for kids to bring candy every day. Taye cries and tries to get it. I hope the community center doesn't give the kids sweets except for special events.

Part 3. Summer Break (Summer 2018)

For me, summer break was a time of travel and study review.

Once Taeju finished her school year, we traveled the Western U.S. for three weeks, late May to the middle of June. We were tired of endless long-distance driving and the bleak landscape of the West, but the journey made us understand America's growth background a little more. And it was nice to have a tour of five beautiful national parks.

In mid-June, my parents and parents-in-law came to the U.S. together. They looked around our hometown of Urbana-Champaign and traveled to Chicago, Springfield, and other Illinois. Taeju and Taye met after a year with their grandparents and had a happy time and showed a lot how well they are.

I was taking parents to Illinois, and I learned a lot more, and most of all, I gained a great deal of support from my parents for my efforts and decisions about studying abroad.

To strengthen the foundation of financial engineering, I reviewed my mathematics study during the day, including calculus, differential equations, and linear algebra, and read the book <Python for Finance> once at night while coding.

Rather than learning English anew, I trained myself to speak English, using the book <Core Pattern 233 of English Conversation> as a reference, so that I could familiarize myself with the expressions.

3.1 U.S. West Car Trip

We left Illinois and returned from a three-week trip through the Western United States. It has 5,330 miles (8,600 kilometers), which is a considerable distance. For your information, it is 5,900 miles from Seoul to Los Angeles. On average, 280 miles (450 kilometers) a day was driven, like from Seoul to Busan every day, and engine oil was replaced at Walmart in Salt Lake City, Utah.

The distance that seemed to be not far on the map was also time-pressed as it was more distant than I thought it would be. Since it was summer, I was able to drive until 8:30 p.m., but we always had 11 a.m. to leave after feeding children's breakfast so that we couldn't afford the schedule. And night driving after dark was avoided as much as possible due to the danger of collision with animals.

Car trip route (clockwise from right end, Illinois)

Although I was tired of endless long-distance driving and the bleak landscape of the West, a big look around the central and western parts of the country, including Route 66, had some sense of the background of American growth and made me understand American people better. And it was even better to see five national parks, called 'America's best ideas.'

This trip consists of five sections.

Section 1. It is a five-day stretch from Illinois to Flagstaff, AZ running west along Route 66.

Section 2. We toured the Grand Canyon, the Bryce Canyon, and the Zion National Park.

Section 3. We came out to Las Vegas, stayed for two days, and then traveled upward to the Salt Lake area, across the Nevada desert.

Section 4. Moved upward from Salt Lake City and looked at Grand Teton, and Yellowstone National Park.

Section 5. The five-day trip from Yellowstone to Cody, WY and back to Illinois via Black Hills, Mount Rushmore, etc.

Many things have been done through rivers and waterways during the two or three hundred years that the United States has been made, although housing and living are now reorganized along motorways. In that sense, the Yellowstone and Grand Teton National Park areas have great significance. These areas are the foothills of the Rocky Mountains that come down from Canada, and the stream that began in many ways stretches like aorta to the Midwest. In other words, Yellowstone and Grand Teton National Park were thought to be the heart of the U.S. continent.

Some water connects to the Yellowstone River and Yellowstone Lake on the right, where they meet with the

Missouri River on the north from North Dakota, and some flow into the strong currents of the Snake River coming down to Grand Teton, stretching out into left Idaho and out into the Pacific Ocean. The waters southward formed the Green River and merged with the Colorado River to create the Grand Canyon in Arizona, with some flowing north to Montana and back into the Madison River to meet with the Missouri River again.

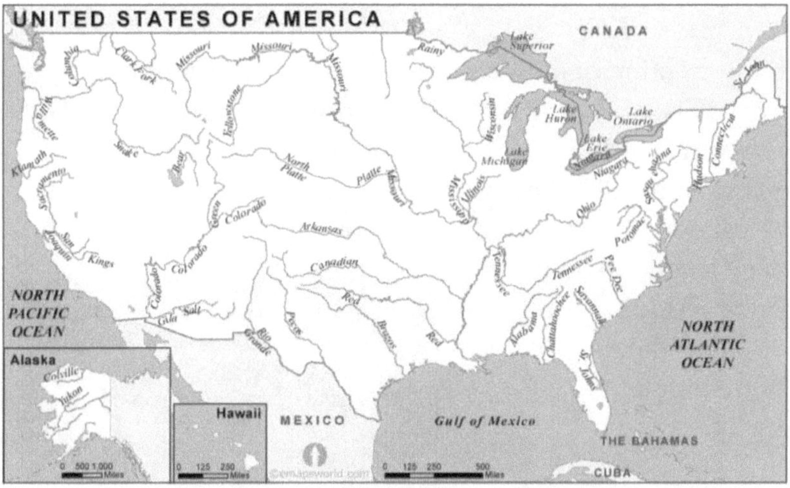

River maps of the United States (emapsworld.com)

The Missouri River, the longest in the U.S., flows far southeast through the plains and meets near St. Louis with the Mississippi River, the lifeline of the U.S., and continues southward, finally joining the sea from New Orleans.

[1] To the West along Route 66

Route 66 is America's first transcontinental highway built in 1926, meaning the California Dream of the United States. In the 1930s, extreme dust storms and droughts, 'Dust Bowl' swept through the Midwest plains for years, and many people rode the Route 66 in search of new life in the West. And after the end of World War II, more relaxed people filled the road with cars traveling west to Las Vegas and Grand Canyon.

With the creation of an interstate highway in 1956 under President Eisenhower to meet the surging demand for roads after World War II, Route 66 completely disappears from the road system in 1985. The way was restored in 2003 under the name 'Historic Road,' but it is still not wholly connected and is not easy to find. And it's a narrow road that can't pick up speed compared to the Interstate Highway.

In other words, Route 66 is a so-called 'mother road' still deeply embedded in the nostalgia of Americans, which was in its heyday until the late 1950s. It succeeded the Western era of the 1800s, the Great Depression of the 1920s and 30s, and then the Interstate Highway was built after World War II.

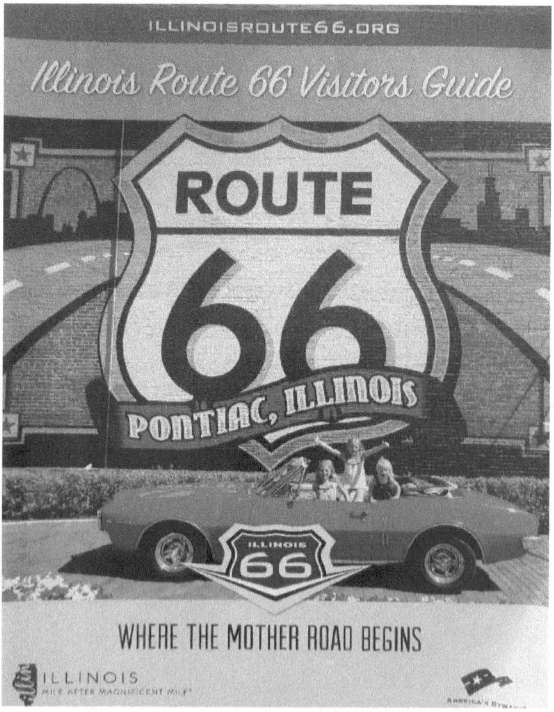

Illinois Rout 66 Visitors Guide

We had a long way to go, so we had to follow Route 66 roughly, but mainly on the interstate highway. Instead, we stopped by the Route 66 Museum and stayed at a motel filled with nostalgia for the Route 66. And in many sections of the west, there was a feeling of running together, as Route 66 was seen beside the interstate highway. A mobile app 'Route 66: Ultimate Guide' helped me find a place to visit.

Illinois

Chicago, Illinois is the place where Route 66 begins. It's about 2,500 miles from the Art Institute of Chicago to the beaches of Santa Monica, California. We started from Springfield, Illinois, near Champaign to save time.

I drove for about two hours from Champaign and arrived in front of Springfield's Union Station. As it was built in the late 19th century and used as a train station until the early 1970s, Lincoln, who died in 1865, would not have been able to use it when traveling to and from Springfield. It is now used as a visitor center to support the Lincoln Memorial and the Lincoln Memorial Library.

Union Station in Springfield, Illinois

In front of Union Station, there is a large park with picnic tables and a sunshade. There is also a convenient way to park on the side of the road, so it is perfect for taking a rest. The bench where Lincoln, made of copper, is sitting is attracting people's attention.

A bench with Lincoln

We walked around the old state Capitol nearby. There were many traces of Lincoln's time in politics, so my wife liked this place. But my children climbed up to the statue and made me nervous. It's a statue of Lincoln's political rival, Stephen Douglas, in front of the House. Lincoln served mostly as a congressman in that room, losing to Douglas in 1859 in the federal Senate elections, but winning the presidential nomination in 1960. It is interesting that at that time, there were not only the Senate and the House but also the legislative, administrative, and judicial branches all together in one building.

Lincoln Presidential Library

Statue of Stephen Douglas, Lincoln's long-time political rival

Missouri

St. Louis is a gateway to the West, both historically and currently on the road system. After living in a quiet city like Urbana, when we entered a big city like St. Louis, people were driving toughly and heard horn sounds often. I ran along the Mississippi River, looking at the gateway arch in the distance. The overpass coming in from outside the city was a dull gray feeling, and there was no open atmosphere like the Han River in Seoul. It was just a crowded and untapped feeling of the city.

We were supposed to go to sleep in Lebanon, Missouri on the first day, so we had to run without even seeing anything in St. Louis. On the way to the highway, Taeju wanted to take a pee and urged me to go faster about 30 times and managed to drop her off to the bathroom. But by the evening, she called about 20 times again to take a poop. After a while, she said she was fine, so I just passed by the Rest Area, but soon after, I was pressed to pull over as she needed pooping again.

Taye is wearing diapers, so he doesn't have this problem, but when he walks into a store or a place, he goes around touching things. He paces around, glancing his eyes around, trying to reach one more thing before parents stop him.

Taeju and Taye's favorite item is QT (Quick Trip) ice cream. They used to urge me to fill the gas because convenience stores were attached to gas stations. Because of the high mileage, I had to enter a gas station once or twice a day. But the QT brand was no

QT store in St. Louis

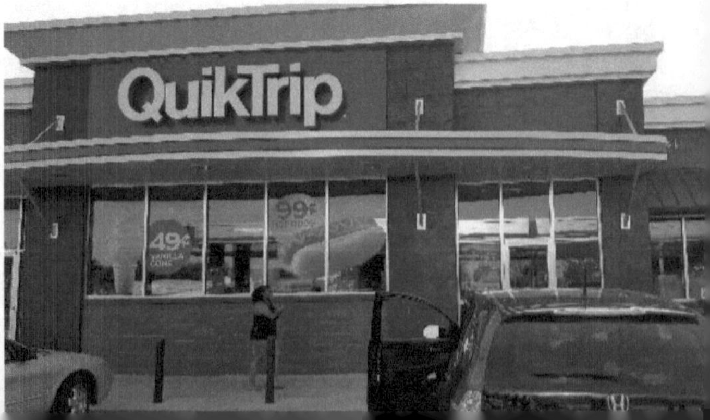

longer seen as we moved west and seems to be only in Missouri and Iowa.

On the first day, we ran until the sun went down and arrived at the Munger-Moss Motel, called the Holy Land of the Route 66 travelers. Munger and Moss are the last names of couples first opened this motel in 1936. It has been operating in its current locations since 1946, with a slight change in the position since World War II. It is said that the current owner, an old lady, bought it in 1971.

Munger-Moss motel, the Holy Land of the Route 66 travelers

I didn't make a reservation because I didn’t expect it to be crowded, but it seemed like more than 40 rooms were almost full. Since there was no two-bedroom, we laid an air mat on the floor in the one-bedroom and put the children to sleep. The price was around 60 dollars and less high than expected, but after experiencing several places, including Motel 6, we thought that it lacks competitiveness a little in terms of facilities, room size, and cleanliness. Also, we were not in a position to feel the nostalgia of Route 66 while talking to our host grandmother, so we didn't have to be tied up in motels called 'Holy Land' in the future.

The next morning, we stopped by the Route 66 Library in Lebanon, but the parking lot was empty and closed. We started this trip on Saturday, today is Sunday, and the next Monday is Memorial Day, so it was a series of holidays. I belatedly realized that this weekend, with Memorial Day, was the peak of high demand for lodging in the United States.

Memorial Day is the last Monday in May, every year. Since universities close their spring semester in mid-May and elementary, middle and high school students start their summer break around the end of May, Memorial Day tends to be the beginning of the summer vacation season in the U.S.

Fortunately, during the hot weather, I found a fountain park that my children liked in Springfield, Missouri. It is a park called Jordan Valley, where children from the neighborhood came with their parents and were playing in the water of the fountain. In the middle, Taye took off all his clothing and played naked, and was protested by American aunts. Taeju was warned again by pulling bricks that had been laid deliberately on the floor out of the water.

Jordan Valley fountain park in Springfield, Missouri

Kansas

Kansas is the home of Dorothy, the hero of <The Wizard of Oz>, but in the case of Route 66, it's all about sneaking across Kansas. And the Kansas Grand Plains are a tornado-prone area that blows up Dorothy's house. Kansas is where the transcontinental bike route, Trans-America Trail, passes rather than Route 66.

Oklahoma

We shopped at Tulsa Walmart and bought a fried chicken and ate it at a nearby park. It already looked more than half Hispanic and sounded Spanish everywhere.

Walmart in Tulsa, Oklahoma

We also saw a car accident on Interstate 44 bound for Oklahoma City from Tulsa. A car rolled over and crumpled several times, lying on its stomach, and a Sonata sedan standing in front of it. Seeing the injured being carried to the ambulance, I thought it was scary. It is a high-speed driving of more than 75 miles (120 kilometers) and roads has a lot of large cargo trucks, which can cause a severe accident once an accident occurs.

Most highways in the U.S. are freeways, but we met two toll roads in Oklahoma, one of which made the mistake of passing on the 'Pike Pass Only Lane.' Pike Pass is like Korea's High Pass. It was late to recognize that it was an exclusive lane and failed to change the paths.

Later, after the trip, the mail was sent home for the violation. It was not a fine, but a simple warning, and it was a marketing-purpose announcement that it would be convenient to install Pike Pass. My wife was wondering whether they would not collect the passage fee, let alone the fine because the previous regular passage cost was about five dollars.

We slept a night at Motel 6 in Oklahoma City and went out to see the State House. The Capitol's doors were closed under construction and happened to see hundreds of motorcycles coming in front of the Capitol. It's like people from nearby local motorcycle clubs who came to attend Memorial Day events here on the grass.

A motorcyclist parade at the state Capitol, Oklahoma City

Thanks to these motorcycles, my family was invited to attend Memorial Day events in Oklahoma City, taking a seat on the lawn and sharing the entire ceremony. It was impressive to see a black female soldier sing the Star-Spangled Banner, a national anthem of the United States.

Memorial Day event in Oklahoma City

In Oklahoma, in addition to the Route 66 sign, there were many other names called 'Will Rogers' - Will Rogers Park, Will Rogers Airport, etc. Even in front of the Route 66 Museum in Oklahoma, there is his memorial stone.

In the 1930s, many Oklahoma people left for western California in search of a new life. As previously described, they moved to the weather-beaten west coast after years of drought in the central plains of Oklahoma.

Oklahoma Route 66 Museum

Will Rogers was a famous comedian, movie star

and playwright from Oklahoma who seems to have been an optimist for life itself, along with an affection for Route 66. In honor of him, it is said to call Route 66 the 'Will Rogers Highway.' Before entering Oklahoma City, there was the Will Rogers Memorial in Claremore, but I'm sorry I didn't see it.

We had lunch at a quiet softball stadium in a small city, Clinton. The only place to avoid the sun in the vast park was the stands for softball. It's good that we didn't show anyone carrying an electric rice cooker. However, it was hard to feed the children because of the strong wind.

Stands in a softball stadium, Clinton, Oklahoma

Texas

Philips 66 Station is one such building as a small hut that you wouldn't know without a smartphone app. It is the first Phillips 66 station in Texas, built in the 1920s at Route 66 in McLean, Texas. Philips 66 is a U.S. oil refinery and distribution company and can be thought as the Route 66's dedicated gas station. Since there weren't enough gas stations in those days,

Americans who were passing through Texas looking for the West probably stopped by.

It's the big dog next door who welcomed us first. Taeju and Taye ran away because they were afraid, but the dog was more likely to follow. On the other side of the street, a couple doing things like a used appliance shop waved to us and kindly greeted us to be good at traveling. Perhaps people visit this place often by watching smartphone apps.

Philips 66 station in McLean, Texas

We stayed at Amarillo Motel 6 and stopped by Amarillo Zoo on Tuesday morning, May 29. The zoo was small in size, but overall it was worth seeing, with tigers and bears, and pretty deer stalking us.

But we felt itchy that day, so I thought a mosquito bit me at the zoo. Later, I came to think of it, the sheets in Amarillo Motel 6 were a little messy, and I saw a white, narrow, rice-like shell, and I think there was probably bedbug. I didn't even know what bedbug was at the time, so I just had a rough sleep, but I think we needed an instant demand, like asking to change them if the sheets are dirty. Anyway, after the trip, we carried out extensive washing and sunburn.

Siberian tigers in Amarillo Zoo

One thing I heard is that in hot, humid regions such as Florida, there are insects called sand-fly, which is very itchy when bitten. Maybe it's a sand-fly. There's a lot of sand in the zoo. As I remember, it was itchier than a mosquito bite.

There is also a place called Cadillac Ranch in Amarillo, where dozens of old cars are blooming on the ground in the middle of a rattling field. It is a sculpture of public art set up in 1974, and although it is privately owned, the view is free. There are many paint lacquers all around, but still hard to find any paint left in it. Fortunately, my wife found one and painted our names on the car.

Cadillac Ranch

A restaurant called Big Texan was famous in Amarillo. It was a renowned place for betting on devouring a lot of steaks quickly, so we didn't visit because it didn't suit us. In the United States, it seemed that the people who reside in Texas were called a Texan.

New Mexico

Santa Rosa's Blue Hole was deep and mysterious. I thought of it as a view of the small waterfalls with clear water, but there were only people who were diving in swimsuits. My kids and I changed into swimsuits, and I even went diving. The water is as cold as ice, and the depth of the water is impossible to tell from the picture.

Blue Hole of Santa Rosa, New Mexico

There were many young people from nearby villages who came to dive. One interesting fact was that no one would swim by crawl stroke like me wearing water glasses. Most of them put their heads entirely out of the water and used easy floating swimming techniques. But it wasn't easy for me because it would sink right away if I didn't keep stirring in the water.

The Blue hole is over 80 feet deep and has a bell shape, so it is narrow above and wide below. In 2016, a diver specializing in underwater caves died while exploring the Bluehole's cave.

After only sleeping in motels for a few days, Taeju sang a song that she wanted to sleep in a tent, so I found RV park in Albuquerque. RV stands for Recreational Vehicle, which is often met on trips in the U.S.

I thought RV park was a cozy camping place for tents, too. By the way, many RV trucks were standing on a level surface like a dune and even many who were shabby in a rented camping car like long-term inn guests. In other words, it's the right place for long-distance RV campers to park overnight and get water and electricity. But, there seems to be not much value for ordinary car travelers to camp out in tents here.

RV park in Albuquerque

On the other hand, U.S. motels systems such as 'Motel 6,' 'Roadway Inn,' and 'Econo Lodge' are reasonable accommodations optimized for car travel. It is a two-story building, and in the case of the first floor, you can put your car in front of the door and move a lot of luggage to the room quickly. And the flow of human movement to toilets, bathrooms, beds, etc. are conveniently configured for travelers. Most of them also have outdoor swimming pools, so we used them often.

The disadvantage of the motel will be that it will be cut off from the outside world when the door is closed, and there will be no interaction with people around it. We were on a family trip, not alone, and it wasn't too bad because we always arrived late in the evening. However, the most popular form seems to be a trip that comes at the lodge by 5 p.m., having a little chat with people and starts early in the next morning.

Motel 6 room in Albuquerque

Traveling is often helped by people in that area. It is the case with the Science Museum in Albuquerque. It is where an old lady, who was taking a dog for a walk in an antique city park, told me about the museum when I didn't even ask. When we went there, it was free, but it was so fantastic for children that they played without knowing how time went by. Thanks to these little kindnesses, we were able to continue our journey.

Albuquerque Science Museum

We also stopped by the Rex Museum in Gallup. New Mexico Gallup is a small town on Route 66 with a population of about 20,000. The atmosphere was unique, and most of the passers-by seem to be descendants of American Indians. The man who runs the Lex Museum seems kind and considerate, and he is also of Indian descent.

The Rex Museum in Gallup

Arizona

Teepee-tent room and a hero on the movie 'Car'

Another landmark of Route 66 along with the Munger-Moss Motel is the Wigwam Motel, located in Holbrook, Arizona. But this time, we decided to sleep in a Motel 6, just by looking around. The Indian Teepee-tent theme of the motel room was set up outside, and there were many old cars on display at the Holy Land of Route 66.

There was an old sky-blue Cadillac next to the motel office, so my kids were touching it, thinking it was a car on display. However, two young guys at the office suddenly got on the vehicle. They started the car and disappeared into the city with the sound of an old engine that was 50 years old. I didn't expect that car to start and roll.

The office and an old car at the Wigwam Motel

On the west side of the U.S., the word 'desolate' is perfect, and there was only desert-like land where crops cannot grow. Sometimes there are grazing cows, but there is no such thing as a cowboy. The invention of the wired fences eliminates the need for cowboys. In a word, there are no people, no homes, so I think it would be scary if a car breaks down here. Indeed, American vehicles should be the best way to make sure that they are reliable and running without a hitch.

I think the person who lives in this place is too lonely, not peaceful. It would be a little comforting to think of the American West, where you can't see a single person when people in urban life stress you. There will be no such stress here, but I feel scared at night and no matter what, I have no place to ask for help.

A mile-train in Arizona

In the Arizona desert, our car often ran side by side with the train. The U.S. cargo trains were long enough to look as many as 200 cargo compartments, so it is called mile-train. Even if there is a train robbery behind the scenes, the driver will not be able to know. The train was so fast that it was almost like my car running at 75 miles per hour. When Taye sees the train, he says, "Choo Choo Train" and likes it and watches it until he can't see it.

We spent the night in Flagstaff, the last city to climb the Grand Canyon. The scorching weather has continued, but the Flagstaff is quite cool because of its high altitude, so my children couldn't get into the motel pool. Still, I built a body that could withstand hard driving while swimming.

Swimming pool of the motel in Flagstaff

Every motel has an ice maker that makes it a great refrigerator if you carry ice around in an icebox. If you put ice in a plastic bag and put it in an ice box, the ice will stick together and won't melt well.

Flagstaff had clean motels, pleasant weather, and comfortable atmosphere in many ways. Fry's Food, which stopped by to buy food, was excellent, cheap and had various items, so we liked it. Among the carts, there was a racing car version that my kids loved, so I picked up two kids and drove around the mart for a long time.

[2] Grand Canyon, Bryce Canyon, Zion

Grand Canyon National Park

We purchased an annual pass for the national park at the Grand Canyon, our first national park. The price is $80 a year. Usually, it costs $30 to $40 per car to enter a national park, so if you visit more than three places, you need to an annual pass.

Desert View Point in Grand Canyon

Grand Canyon National Park, a leading American star, was simply a spectacular sight. It is hard to believe that the blue Colorado River that flows down has carved out these magnificent canyons. And it's incredible that Native Americans have lived under that canyon for thousands of years. The largest of the many viewpoints, Desert View Point, was near our campground, so it was easy to see.

We set up a tent at the Desert View Campground in the East. We arrived at around 2 p.m., with two or three out of the 50 tent sites remaining. We quickly registered one and prepared a meal. Most of the campsites were reservation-based, so they ended several months ago. Only Desert View campground was a first-come-first-served basis, and it was quieter, cozy, and better than I thought.

Our tent was Amazon's best-selling product last year, even one in the same shape, the same color, was seen nearby. It is good because it is mobile and straightforward, but in cold areas, it is a little short of preventing the early morning cold.

Desert View campground

We toured in the South Rim area, and the far-sighted part of the picture is the North Rim area. Most of the 5 million tourists who visit the Grand Canyon each year come into the South Rim area. The North Rim region is only allowed half of the year due to the cold weather and poor accessibility from large cities such as Las Vegas. That is why the number of tourists is significantly lower than that of the South Rim, which is open year-round.

South Rim area is crowded with many people. It is more convenient because it has many shuttle buses. Mather Point presents a beautiful view that must be seen

Far-sighted North Rim area

with the Desert View Point. Stephen Mather is the first president of the national park and the father of the national park.

In addition to the Desert View, there are several viewpoints such as Navajo Point, Lipan Point, and Grand View Point, which are very dangerous due to the lack of handrails. I couldn't look around comfortably to keep my children away. Some young people are taking pictures and making a fuss at the end of slippery rocks. Did they want to get stimulated because they were having a hard time living? There are newspaper articles that someone lost one's footing and fall to death while taking pictures at the edge of a cliff to post it on social networking sites. There are many other things in the world to be brave except this.

Tusayan Museum and Ruin is a historical site of the Pueblo Indians not too far from Desert View Point. Pueblos, which means village in Spanish, is the name given by the Spanish conquerors when they first came here around 1600, and they saw native people living in what is now Arizona, New Mexico, and Texas. This area has been excavated from the ruins of a Tusayan Pueblo Indian village that lived 800 years ago and showed it in the form of an outdoor museum. There were rooms for ancestral rites called Kiva and food storage. However, it is questionable how corn has grown in such a barren land.

Tusayan Museum at the entrance to the ruins

There is a self-check-in machine in front of the Desert View Campground bathroom. It is a system that first visits any of the empty sites and then comes here to register with a credit card. Even though it's self-check-in, one campground janitor walks around in a small electric car, so you can ask what you are curious about.

Self-Check-in machine in front of bathroom

There was a birds nest in a tree hole right next to our site, and mommy bird kept coming and going in the morning to feed baby birds. Above all, what impressed me was the many stars in the night sky. I used to lie down and watch stars after dinner when I was young, but this is the first time in my life that I've seen so many stars. We spent two nights there because we liked there.

Desert View Campground site no. 21

Bryce Canyon National Park

Saturday, June 2nd, the road to Bryce Canyon from Grand Canyon was also a long way away, taking more than four to five hours. Just before arriving at the Arizona Page, Horseshoe Bend was seen, but due to time considerations, we could not stop by. Furthermore, because my children were young and the weather was hot, it was almost impossible to walk on a trail that required even a little walk. As there was no room in the trunk of the car, I could not bring a trailer to carry my children. We refueled on the Page and went to Bryce Canyon without much sight.

Highway 89 from Grand Canyon

It's smaller than Page, but we have to pass through Kanab to go to Bryce Canyon or Zion National Park. We spread our seats in the back of that fountain and had lunch. The background of the red mountain behind is as exotic as Arizona. But Kanab belongs to Utah by a hair's breadth. Even there exists one hour of the time gap between Page and Kanab.

Rest area in Kanab, Utah

Thinking that the three canyons were relatively close together, I tried to see Bryce Canyon and Zion today, but it was a big miscalculation. By the time we arrived at Bryce Canyon, it was already past 5 p.m., so we had to change our plans and set up a tent at Bryce Canyon for the day. Fortunately, most campsites had a few remained seats if not during the peak season. We settled down at the Sunset campground. It was so cold at night that everyone slept shivering. After that, it was said that Taeju liked motels better than camping tents.

Bryce Canyon Sunset Campground

The Bryce Canyon was great to see deer everywhere, but another unique view, different from the Grand Canyon, was spectacular. A red rock column called hoodoo lined up like a canyon. If the Grand Canyon is erosion by the river, the Hoodoo of the Bryce Canyon is said to have been cut in the process of repeated freezing and melting in the snow or rain.

More than anything else, it was also good for us that most of the attractions are located in a limited area called the Amphitheater. The Grand Canyon is vast and requires a full day's drive only to see some of the sights, but the Bryce Canyon could do more than you thought without much effort.

I would recommend Bryce Canyon if you have to choose only one of the two at a limited time.

Hoodoo of Bryce Canyon

Zion National Park

Sunday, June 3rd. In the morning, we went to Zion National Park, enjoying the hoodoo once again at Bryce Canyon. Once I told uncle Keach before the trip that we were going to national parks, and he recommended that Zion National Park was the best for him.

We entered the East Gate to come from Bryce Canyon. But we were told there was a tunnel accident in the middle and that all traffic was stopped, and two camping cars were trapped. Many cars turned back to the South Gate on rumors that it would take about two hours to recover. Going back is a long distance of nearly two hours, so we just waited and ate lunch in the car, and fortunately, the traffic resumed about an hour later.

Huge rocky cliffs made of Navajo sandstone

Zion National Park was a mysterious place with colossal rocky cliffs lined on both sides. The sheer size of the rock makes it look great for rock climbing, but this is the Navajo sandstone, so it's likely to break down naturally.

Anyway, the best way to travel here is to try walking the trail by dipping your feet in shallow stream-like water. However, we had to be as satisfied as to the Emerald Pond Walkway with young children. And unlike Bryce Canyon, Zion National Park was very hot.

The front seat of the rear compartment is the best place for sightseeing. Taye was also distracted by sight. However, it's not scenery, but the tour bus in front of him.

Front seat of the rear compartment in shuttle bus

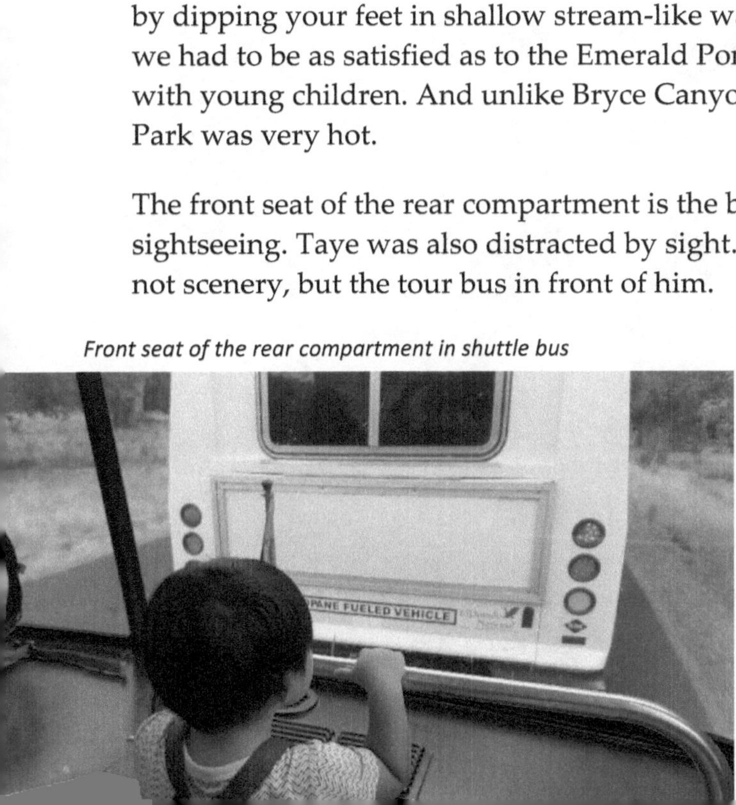

[3] Las Vegas, Salt Lake

Las Vegas

We stayed in Las Vegas for two days on June 3-4. My wife liked it when we went to Las Vegas since we were walking around in the wilderness. There was a lot to see on the street, and we swam and had a comfortable time at the Ellis Island Hotel. It is relatively close to the two blocks on the right at Las Vegas Boulevard, the center of Las Vegas tourism. Las Vegas has many hotels, so it is very cheap for the quality.

I was looking for a place to park for free and play for children when I heard the Circus Circus Hotel is excellent for it. As a city of gambling, children's play was seen as a lot of gambling.

There was a music fountain show at the Bellagio Hotel at night. Music is good, and above all, the water particles from the wind cool the summer night.

Bellagio Hotel music fountain show

A volcano show at the Mirage Hotel was excellent. It's hot for a moment when a volcano erupts, but it's worth seeing. There is also the Eiffel Tower in Las Vegas. Taeju wanted to eat ice cream, so we searched for a long time for a store to sell. Taye keeps asking me to hold him if he walks a little bit, so I can't walk much. It's a pity that we couldn't bring a bike trailer because of the heavy load.

Volcano show at the Mirage Hotel

Venetian Las Vegas Hotel was modeled after the Venetian Canal. The gondola boatman was singing Italian songs to passengers.

Another impressive thing about Las Vegas was a huge Korean mart called Greenland a little bit outside. Various products are being sold at low prices that are incomparably different from Champaign Korean mart. There were also many side dishes made by themselves. It must be a sign that many Koreans are living in Las Vegas.

Salt Lake

Tuesday, June 5th, we gave up Yosemite and headed straight north from Las Vegas to Wendover. June 14th is the day my parents arrive from Korea, and I didn't think we can return to Illinois until that day if we go west anymore.

With the boundaries of Nevada and Utah, the atmosphere of the city itself was strange, as well as a salt mass. However, here motel 6 is one of the cleanest, most convenient, and inexpensive places to stop at this trip. The road across the Nevada desert was bleaker than Arizona. Arizona can sometimes see grazing cattle, but Nevada is all yellow desert land except for the palm-like cactus. The U.S. has a vast estate, but not much valuable area.

Wendover Motel 6 view

Wendover has an immense Bonneville Salt Flats, making it look like a white snowfield. When it rains in spring or fall, the salt plain shines and is said to be truly spectacular.

The highway from Wendover to Salt Lake City was as flat as a plain, straight line with a speed limit of 85 miles. It is a fast speed of nearly 140 kilometers per hour. But it was a vast expanse of plains, so I didn't feel any speed. It is called the Autobahn of the United States and is used as a test road for various vehicles.

Wendover's endless salt plains, Bonneville Salt Flats

I've been running for a long time, and I've been nagged at the dashboard to change engine oil before long. I was thinking about changing the oil after arriving at Illinois, but I checked the engine oil with a dipstick and decided to change it during the trip because of its poor color and inadequate viscosity. An oil change was made at a Walmart, south of Salt Lake City. I was going to do it for the cheapest one (29.98 dollars), but the mechanic recommended that I should use synthetic oil for this car, so I just did it. (44.88 dollars)

Salt Lake City has a Mormon headquarters called Temple Square and is also famous for its tourist attractions. The sun was so hot that Taeju took a picture hiding in the shade.

Oil change in a Walmart, Salt Lake City

There is a large pipe organ in front of the church. In Salt Lake City or Utah, the signboard Zion Bank also frequently seen. When I think of it, there was the mount Zion in the lyrics of the song in my church.

Giant pipe organ in Temple Square

The next day, there was a long way to go to the Grand Teton National Park, so we moved a little further northeast of Salt Lake City and stayed at a place called Evanston. It was already a high-altitude area, so the climate was cool and rainy and even fickle. Perhaps because it is cold here, the windowed form is also less open compared to the southern region.

Motel 6 in Evanston, Utah

[4] Grand Teton, Yellowstone

Grand Teton National Park

Thursday, June 7th. On our way up from Evanston to Jackson, we took a little turn as we looked around with Bear Lake on our right. Lake Bear, which spans Idaho and Utah, was quite beautiful as a lake with the legend of monster living. There were some marine sports resorts around the big lake, which was hard to escape.

Taye, who dipped his feet in Lake Bear

While we had lunch at a picnic table next to a quiet neighborhood playground, I felt the comfortable life that the ancients talked about seems to be here in Idaho.

We arrived at Jackson, the gateway city of Grand Teton National Park, and rested in the Town Square. The elk-horn arches that we used to see on TV were in four ways, and tempted us to take pictures. Taeju looked inside, but it was not only made of elk-horn but also has a skeleton structure inside.

Elk-horn arches in Town Square

As we go up to Grand Teton National Park from Jackson, we can see a place called Jackson Hole, where arriving planes are seen. That is the place the annual Jackson Hole meeting, where central bank governors and economists from all over the world are gathered, is held.

Scenery entering Grand Teton

We stopped by Jenny Lake, which has the best view in the park and checked the campground situation at the visitor center. Jenny Lake Campground is said all seats were filled and there were still seats in Colter Bay campground in the north and Gros Ventre campground in the south. We arrived late in the afternoon because we were on the move all day, so we had no choice.

Jenny Lake is much smaller than Jackson Lake in the north, but the snow-capped Teton peaks behind the lake are closer than Jackson Lake, showing a Swiss-looking background. The name Grand Teton means 'big breast' in French and is given by first-time French fur traders in this area, but I didn't think it looks exactly alike.

Colter Bay campground is near Jackson Lake, and there is a big store nearby, so it is convenient. But there were too many mosquitoes because of the thick forest. It's okay to go into the tent and rest, but when you eat dinner at the table, you can't eat unless you spray mosquito repellent. In comparison, the Grand Canyon campground seems to have been dry and desolate in itself, so there were no mosquitoes. Colter Bay was an excellent place to burn firewood at night to chase mosquitoes and melt bodies, but I couldn't prepare for the trip during the day and tried to borrow it from a nearby tent.

Our tent put up in Colter Bay Campground

We spent two days at the Colter Bay Campground, and we also went to Yellowstone from here. Colter Bay is north of Grand Teton, and it's a hassle to put up and take down a tent in a day, so I went to Yellowstone by using Colter Bay as a base camp. But more than I thought, Yellowstone was too big that it was quite burdensome to watch and come back to Colter Bay. It was the wrong choice.

I could see various camping cars here and there at the camping site. I had to open and fold the tent and air mat by myself, so I felt the most desirable type is a mobile camping car like the photo. It was even a Benz. A large vehicle with a bathroom and

Mercedes-Benz camping car

shower inside a camping car is a little onerous. The camping car I want is that I can spread out the bed and lie down right away when I'm tired of travel, and then fold back, and move again.

I saw a rooftop tent that put a tent on top of the car, but it seems to be a labor to install, and most of all, the kids can't walk up the ladder.

Colter Bay Campground was near Jackson Lake but was hiding the lake. I came down the forest path next to the campsite for 2-3 minutes, and a beautiful view was waiting for me. There is also a picnic table next to it, so I don't think there will be an any better place to watch the scenery over lunch.

The Chapel of the Transfiguration is a small church at the south entrance of the National Park. Before the chapel was built here in 1925, residents had to go all the way to Jackson to give Mass. The size is small, but it is overwhelming to see the picturesque Teton peaks through the large windows behind the podium.

Chapel of Transfiguration in Grand Teton National Park

It was great to this point, but as I left the south gate to get to Yellowstone National Park, I got a speeding ticket on a quiet eastern road. I was awarded a speeding ticket for 65 miles on a 45-mile speed limit, with a fine of $200 and a processing fee of $30, totaling $230.

U.S. police car having the stealth function

In the U.S., there is little camera speed control, but police cars are often waiting behind the scenes, and fines are very heavy if they are caught. And the police cars were barely indistinguishable from regular SUVs, so they didn't even know until they stuck behind me to light up and squealed. If you look at the white car in the picture, the warning light unit itself is transparent and flat, so it may not be identified until they turn it on. It seems to have introduced stealth technology of fighter jets to police cars as well.

Yellowstone National Park

Yellowstone, the first national park in the U.S. and the world's first, was huge. People tour along an eight-character road called the Grand Loop, but it's hard to get around an eight-character loop even if you drive all day. In other words, at least two nights or three days are needed to see the park properly. On Friday, June 8th, I took the first driving shift with my wife because I had accumulated driving fatigue as I went around the whole loop in one day.

The area, which is larger than all of Korea's national parks combined, has magma in deep underground, which smells like sulfur and is dotted with hot springs and geysers. If hot springs are pools of hot spring water, a geyser is referred to a spot where steam and gas are pumped up, and if the water is not boiling, it is just called a pool. This hydrothermal phenomenon is a unique characteristic of Yellowstone among other national parks. The smell of sulfur was very similar to the scent when I made boiled eggs out of a rice cooker at home.

Yellowstone National Park has four entrances, east, west, north, and south, and most tourists who want to see the national parks of Arizona and Utah, usually get off at Salt Lake City Airport in Utah and drive for five to six hours into the West entrance. Yellowstone or Grand Teton belong to the Rocky Mountains and is much north of the three canyons, so the weather is cold and the accessibility from big cities is not so good.

We stopped at the Grand Teton first and then went up through the South entrance to Yellowstone, so an area called West Thumb first appeared. It's a thumb-shaped area west of Yellowstone Lake, and the surrounding sapphire-like geysers are worth seeing. For safety reasons, all wooden decks have been built.

Yellowstone's hot springs are a dangerous place where humans cannot immerse themselves due to temperatures of more than 100 degrees Celsius, and there have been 22 deaths since 1870. Most recently, in 2016, an American man in his 20s who was touring the Norris region's hot springs slipped and died while trekking over a wooden fence. From Oregon, a brother and sister came to watch and tried to reach out to see if they could take a bath. The rescue team was immediately sent there by the sister's report. But he had already died, and as it tried to salvage him the next day due to bad weather, he was said to have been dissolved in the acid hot spring water.

Unlike Norris, West Thumb is close to a lake, so the water is not that hot. Black Pool is a result of the cold water and the abundance of dark-colored bacteria, which changed in 1991 and suddenly became hot, causing black bacteria to die and become the sapphire color of the present day, but the name is still black.

Black Pool of West Thumb

We waited nearly an hour to see the eruption of Old Faithful but felt empty. To exaggerate that high expectations are disappointing, it was hard for me to find more meaning than a fountain in the neighborhood park. What is different from other geysers is that the eruptions cycle is about 90 minutes constant, so it's even called 'faithful.' Once vented, it was believed to have been 20 to 30 meters of water and two minutes in time.

Explosion of Old Faithful

One surprising fact is that in Yellowstone, there were more than a thousand earthquakes a year, and the 1959 earthquake blocked the Madison River's waterways toward Montana, leaving a large earthquake lake and making dozens of campers missing. At this time, water vapor, which usually comes at an hour and a half interval from Old Faithful 100 kilometers away, came up all day.

We met a group of bison while we were traveling in a car. Many mother bison have babies that are about the size of calves that look like it was born in spring. Most of the safety accidents here in Yellowstone are related to bison. It seems gentle, but in reality, it is violent, and since it weighs close to a ton, people can be seriously injured, so bison is banned from access.

A group of bison moving along the Nez Perce Creek

Bison was everything to the American Indians. Meat became food, hair became warm clothes, and leather was the material for building Indian Teepee Tent. The bison population, which stood at more than 40 million at the end of the 18th century, was left less than 100 at the end of the 19th century due to the

Moving bison panoramic photo

ruthless hunting of white people to take away the Indian's living foundation. Since then, after restoration efforts, including the designation of Yellowstone as a national park and banning bison hunting, about 5,000 are currently living in Yellowstone.

That river in front of the bison is Nez Perce Creek, and it merges into the Madison River in the northern state of Montana and eventually enters the Missouri River. Nez Perce is a tribal name that has lived here for thousands of years, and there is a painful history of Chief Joseph that his party was fled to Canada in 1877 after a fierce battle with white people, forcing them to surrender.

The Grand Prismatic Spring was located in the Midway Geiser Basin. The Grand Prismatic Spring on the cover of the book my wife bought in the past was fantastic, but in reality, it doesn't look that good. Considering that there is a staircase that goes up the mountain in front, it must have been taken there.

Grand Prismatic Spring panoramic photo

Mammoth Hot Springs Mound Spring

Mammoth Hot Springs area is a natural step created by limewater. A big snake whizzes in front of me as I go down the terrace. It was a big snake that looked scary like a rattlesnake, not like a grass snake. Meanwhile, Taeju is said to have touched it at the zoo, and she said the snake was also cute.

Long way to the east, there was also a picnic area, where you can eat a quiet meal right next to Yellowstone Lake. It was very

A picnic table in front of Yellowstone Lake

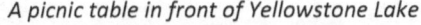

hard to find. It was a Gull Point Drive picnic area. There was no sign of direction, but the atmosphere is so comfortable that some people park a camping car next to the Gull Point and stay all day.

People are looking at something with a telescope while we are driving diligently to get out of Yellowstone. When I asked one of them, she said there was a grizzly bear. I went out with Taeju and looked closely and saw two bears loitering in the woods over there. The grizzly bear is an endangered species, with about 700 remaining in the nearby area.

People watching grizzly bears

The East entrance of Yellowstone National Park was especially an undeveloped sense of wildness. Most of the tourists come through the West entrance and go out again through the West entrance. We could see a lot of wild animals such as bison and deer as we came out this way.

[5] Back to Illinois via the Black Hills

Wyoming

When we came down from Yellowstone, it was already dark and drove as fast as I could to find a motel in Cody, Wyoming. The atmosphere in the village was cowboylike and even a stadium playing rodeo under the night lights. When I woke up the next morning, the wind was so strong that I thought a typhoon was coming, but it seemed like a usual breeze here. The Big Bear Motel we stayed in isn't cheap at $99 a night, but the motels around here are all the same. Looking back, Las Vegas hotels gave the best satisfaction for the price.

Big Bear Motel in Cody, Wyoming

Taye's sneakers were sweaty and smelled like feet, so I washed them myself. When Taye got in the car and took off his sneakers, he used to shout, "baby feet pooping." It means that his feet have a terrible smell. The whole car is full of foot odor, and Taeju is in a hurry to lower the window. I tried to buy him a pair of sandals at Walmart, but he didn't want to wear them.

Sunday, June 10th, at a place called Worland, Wyoming, I was reissued a speeding ticket. It's a $127 fine for driving 43 miles in a town with a speed limit of 30 miles. When I got out of the market, the road had no car, so I ran a little fast naturally. I feel bad that I had to pay for it because I was caught in a trap.

My wife is worried that we may pay 1,000 dollars by the end of our trip if I am not careful. Taeju repeatedly complains that her dad drove fast and got caught again. Since both of speeding tickets were issued in Wyoming, I think I should get out of here as soon as possible. Wyoming seems to cover its budget with a speeding fine.

It's a mountain park called Willow Park, where kids from the neighborhood were camping out. We had a late lunch there. Taeju and Taye also played together, but they looked like rural children and seemed to be curious about a dark-haired Asian.

Play with local kids in Willow Park

South Dakota

We chose the route through the Black Hills because we didn't want to see only the plain on our way back to Illinois as we did when coming. We went all the way to Custer and slept in Roadway Inn. Unlike Motel 6, it's good to give us breakfast. There was a plausible waffle maker, and my wife made some waffles herself for Taeju.

On Monday, June 11th, we had to hurry because it was a town with lots of things to see, but we always leave at 11 a.m., the checkout time, as we have young children. We watched as we passed a statue of Crazy Horse still working on the mountain, then we headed straight for the Wild Loop Road.

The Wild Loop Road is a road where wild animals show up without mercy, where my wife found them on the Internet. But, when we passed by, we could see only birds, so we went to the visitor center to ask. We did not know the exact location of the wild animals because they often moved, but they showed me the area on the map in which animals were roughly there. The visitor center also has an exhibition hall, where we can see the wild sheep Big Horn through the stuffed. It is not easy to be seen in the wild because they usually go over steep mountains.

Near the Wild Loop Road, donkeys (wild burro) also live, but people give them too many snacks, so I am not sure if they will be healthy. In principle, it is forbidden to provide food to wild animals. These wild burros are descended from a group of animals that used to carry luggage on the trail. When people

A wild burro lying down for sleep

pass by in cars, they approach the vehicle for food. Some of them lay down, as if it was too much to eat.

Buffalo was in remote fields and looked scary, so people couldn't get close and didn't even give snacks. I wanted to pat the buffalo, but I put up with it because I had work to do back in Illinois.

A swarm of buffalo grassing in the field

When Europeans first came to America, they thought that American bison was similar to buffalo in Africa or Asia, so they used in mixed with bison and buffalo. I looked carefully because people here called it buffalo, and I think it has a slightly smaller head and a more prominent horn than the bison I saw in Yellowstone.

The cutest star on the Wild Loop Road is prairie dogs. It sticks his head out of a crooked hole in the field, and when a man approaches, it escapes into the ground and comes out of another hole. There are hundreds of them out in the area. The color is yellow like a puppy, so pictures don't flatter to prairie dogs than the actual cuteness.

Mount Rushmore National Memorial

I drove again to the Mount Rushmore National Memorial. We didn't expect much because we passed the statue of Crazy Horse, but Rushmore's sculptures of presidents were grand. There is no entrance fee, but need to pay $11 for parking.

George Washington, the first U.S. president on the left end, and Abraham Lincoln on the right end, with Thomas Jefferson and Theodore Roosevelt in the middle. The statue was made from 1927 to 1941 and given that President Roosevelt delivered a commemorative speech for completion, I think he ordered the work and inserted his face slightly. Thomas Jefferson, the third president, created the U.S. Declaration of Independence and bought Louisiana territory, which is now the Midwest of the U.S., from France, paving the way for the country to explore its vast western region.

I didn't know when I was taking pictures from above, but when I went down, I found a beautiful concert hall hidden down the mountain. If I were a musician, I would like to play in a concert hall like that.

Describing the process of making large sculpture

It is well explained in the memorial how systematically and continuously worked for that task. It took 14 years for workers to hang from a rope and carve it with a hammer and chisel after drawing a sketch. The face length alone is 18 meters, and the mountain itself is high and can be seen from a distance of 100 kilometers. They initially tried to carve not just the face but the whole body, but ended up sculpting only the face due to budget shortages.

During the trip, our children always come close to dogs because they want to touch a dog when it appears. Then, most Americans take the time for kids to feel their dog, saying it is friendly and doesn't bite.

From Mount Rushmore, we came out to Rapid City and took a quick look at Dinosaur Park. I had to follow a sky road so that We could see the downtown of Rapid City at a glance.

The dinosaurs are made of real size and have explanations on the bottom, but Taeju and Taye are focused on riding them. Triceratops is a plant-eating animal of a three-horned, four-legged species.

Rhino-like triceratops

Tyrannosaurus, by contrast, is the predatory dinosaur's best-ever, short-footed, the evolution of theropod. It says that it weighs eight tons.

Many traces of T-rex eating the triceratops remain on the fossil. Triceratops appears to have evolved a big horn to counter the Tyrannosaurus. Both are dinosaurs that lived 65 million years ago and existed in South Dakota.

Tyrannosaurus vs. Triceratops

The night drive was inevitable as the departure to the hotel was delayed due to many sightseeing. On our way to Mitchell, he had a quick dinner with hamburgers and egg rolls at the Highway Travel Center. The Travel Center is also dropped by a lot of truck drivers who drive all day, so it brings some things that might be a meal. The cars lined up in the parking lot were all large cargo trucks.

Corn Palace in Mitchell is a corn-themed children's museum. You could ride it directly on a corn harvesting machine. Then we arrived at Sioux Falls. We visited Falls Park to take a rest after lunch.

Lewis and Clark Memorial, heroes of the American West Pioneer, are in Sioux City. Sioux Falls or Sioux City are cities on the Missouri River, and Sioux is a local Indian tribal name that the French gave to them as they explored along the Missouri River. Later, Napoleon sold Louisiana to Thomas

Lewis & Clark Memorial in Sioux City

Jefferson for money, which enabled Western reclamation and now has the vast U.S. In fact, Lewis and Clark's expedition to the West came shortly after the Louisiana Purchase, ordered by President Thomas Jefferson.

Nebraska

It is in front of Warren Buffett's house. He is called a wise man, value investment guru. Taeju suddenly pressed the intercom, so we were embarrassed. Since it already happened, I asked for a look at the garden once, but was rejected by a man believed to be Warren Buffett's voice.

Warren Buffett didn't put us to bed, so we spent the night at the Best Western Hotel in Omaha instead. There was the University of Nebraska in downtown Omaha, and the playground in the Elmwood park next to the university has many toys.

Warren Buffett's Omaha home

Iowa

In Iowa City, we went to the Children's Museum to go to the bathroom and rest. There were many amusement facilities, including a cafeteria, inside the building decorated like a shopping mall.

Children's Museum in Iowa City

Illinois

I couldn't confirm the gas at the thought of coming near my house, but there was a gas lamp already on. I had to run a long way to the next exit where the gas station was located, and even though I followed the exit, the gas station was nowhere to be seen. While wandering for a long time, I found a gas station and convenience store in a village called Brimfield. I breathed a sigh of relief at a time when I almost stopped on the highway because I was running out of gas at night. However, there is still a gate called Peoria and Bloomington to the house.

Usually, I'd stop by Peoria and Bloomington for some rest, but it's already past nine o'clock at night. In the middle of the break, we ate a dish, and Taye enjoyed a great deal of pooping. When I check the instrument panel after arriving home at 11 o'clock, it shows a total of 5,337 miles on this trip.

The gas station attached to the general store

Thank you for running so well, Black Honda!

3.2 Travel to Illinois

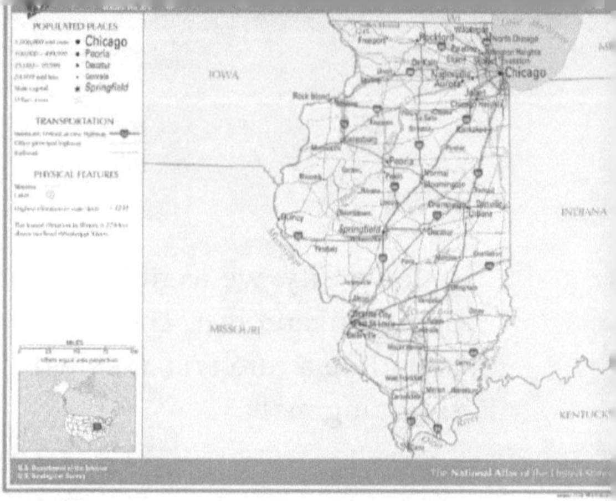

Illinois State map (nationalatlas.gov)

This summer, my parents and parents-in-law from Korea visited our home in Illinois together for ten days. I was able to drive around Illinois for the first time in a long time, and I could see and feel many things I didn't know even though I lived for nearly a year.

The name 'Illinois' comes from the native tribal name of the region, Illiniwek, and, as many geographical names in the central part of the U.S., is a phonetic alphabet of American Indian words in French. On the left, Illinois borders Iowa and Missouri on the Mississippi River and the south, Kentucky on the Ohio River. The population became the fifth largest state in the United States thanks to Chicago, and the land is fertile and all flat, so most of the property grows corn and soybeans. I've never seen a mountain anywhere in Illinois.

The license plate of Illinois says, Land of Lincoln. Abraham Lincoln, the 16th president of the United States, was born in Kentucky in the south, but he often mentioned Illinois as his hometown, where he grew up, engaged in political activities, and buried. It was also the first U.S. state to legislate for the liberation of black slavery in 1865.

First, I visited the Champaign-Urbana region, including the University of Illinois, and then Chicago, one of the top three cities in the United States. I've felt Lincoln's traces in Springfield, the town of Lincoln, and I've been on a cruise ship in Peoria, the representative city of the Illinois River. I was sorry to pass Decatur only by car. After my parents went back to Korea, I took time to revisit Decatur for a day.

[1] Champaign-Urbana

The name of the university is Urbana-Campaign, but when indicating this area, it is usually referred to as Champaign-Urbana. It is also called Chambana for short. Urbana was a bigger city, but ironically, rail traffic has opened to the Champaign area, which used to be the western outskirts of Urbana, and it is now much more extensive than Urbana.

Orchard Downs and Arboretum

When we came back from the three-week trip to the West, we had a lot of laundries, including blankets, sleeping bags, and clothes. The laundry room has dozens of washing machines and dryers, and various amenities, including drinking water tables, vending machines, and ice machines. The dryer must be turned for more than 90 minutes in case of bedding to dry completely. It's a bit of a hassle to have a person move it to the dryer oneself when the laundry is finished. If the smartphone application is installed, the progress of each laundry machine can be monitored. The bulletin board is equipped with various announcements, so it is also necessary to stop by regularly.

Orchard Downs laundry room

Inside the Arboretum, there is the Japan House. It seems to be run by the university's liberal arts college. There are some rooms where you can drink tea, and you can also see Japanese-style house gardens at the front and back. This year marks the

20th anniversary of its formal installation and is also a typical dating course for University of Illinois students, including a nearby walkway.

There are some big birds that flies around with the noise of a pig. I didn't know the exact name, so I called it a piggy bird, but it turned out to be a Canada Goose. Native to North America and relatively well adapted to urbanization, it has a large population throughout North America. There is a big pond in front of the Japan House, so these birds often fly in. The cubs are so cute that they're not entirely white, but they're mixed with brown.

Canada geese couple with a large number of cubs

A group of horse riders was walking through the Arboretum forest. There were five women, and I think they're riding a horse for exercise. In Seoul, I saw a horse riding in the playground of an elementary school on Sunday morning. Compared to that, Arboretum is a perfect place. It is a forest and garden managed by the university, and it is a view from our living room because it is adjacent to the Orchard Downs.

Women riding horses in the Arboretum

On the day my parents stayed for ten days and left for Korea again, my children said goodbye in front of our home. They had a lot of trouble getting in the car and not coming. Taeju is old enough to know the meaning of parting and Taye seems to follow his older sister, though he doesn't know yet.

Meadowbrook Park, Crystal Lake Park

Meadowbrook Park is a treasure trove of our town. There is a large wooden playground that children love, and it is also suitable for taking dogs for a walk. It's about halfway down to the Meijer mart.

Meadowbrook Park in Urbana

Crystal Lake Park is another gem-like park we've found. It's in the northern part of Urbana, and there's a big lake called Crystal Lake, and a water boat. It's good to have lunch with kids playing as playgrounds are in large public spaces, and there are many picnic tables. Hundreds of piggy birds (Canada Goose) are playing in droves here. The trees are so thick that they are estimated to have been planted more than 150 years ago when the city was first built. For your information, the University of Illinois was founded in 1867 and celebrated its 150th-anniversary last year.

Dr. King elementary school

The official name of the Taeju's school is Dr. Martin Luther King, Jr. Elementary School, which is commonly referred to as King School. My parents and parents-in-law said during their visit to the United States that it was most impressive to see Taeju studying in the King School and that they would never forget it.

A teacher who guides us in King school

We happened to stop by King school to see Taeju, but a teacher showed us around the school, and we could see Taeju taking a summer school at the gym. We were able to pass by and attend an art classe. In particular, this teacher praised Taeju for being good at rock climbing.

Attending an art class

Engineering Quad (mechse.illinois.edu)

University of Illinois

Quad, Grainger Library, Engineering Hall

First, we looked around the engineering quad. Engineering school is where I usually take classes and study. Quad is an abbreviation for quadrangle, which refers to a courtyard surrounded by buildings in college. The University of Illinois has a total of three quads: Main Quad, Engineering Quad, and South Quad, of which the Engineering Quad is in the north.

The engineering quad is also called the Bardeen quad, which commemorates John Bardeen, who has been a professor at the University of Illinois Engineering school for nearly 40 years since 1951. He is said to have been the only person to win the Nobel Prize in Physics twice as the father of semiconductor history, but also a very humble man. It was John Bardin, a doctoral advisor of Nick Holonyak, who first invented LEDs in 1965.

The Grainger Engineering Library, the northern boundary of the engineering quad, is the most extensive engineering library in the United States. Grainger, a 1919 graduate, became a billionaire in Fortune 500, with a company named W. W. Grainger, an industrial parts distributor he created. It is currently listed on the New York Stock Exchange (NYSE) under the name GWW and is also included in the S&P 500.

So, this is a library made in 1994 by Grainger's donation. There is a statue at the entrance that is always sitting and reading a book. Like the engineering library, the title is 'Computing the Future.' I took a picture of my family next to the statue.

Reading Man in Grainger Library

Illini Union

Illini Union building is the equivalent of a student center. On the other hand, there is an Illini Hotel and a restaurant and bowling alley underground. The Asiana Airline shuttle that goes back and forth to Chicago will take you down right there. It departs Chicago's O'Hare Airport at 8:30 p.m. from Terminal 5, Parking Lot D, and from Union here at 5:00 p.m. The Chicago Sharp Travel Agency signed a five-year contract with Asiana Airline, which unfortunately only runs until January 2019.

Illini Union building

ARC (Activities & Recreation Center)

We also stopped by the ARC, one of the university gyms. The outdoor swimming pool was good to see in the cool lobby without having to enter the gym. I've been swimming before, and it felt like a 50-meter lane was longer than I thought. And there was a diving pool next to it, so it was useful to practice. You have to carry a personal padlock to use the locker, and you have to take care of the towels.

ARC outdoor swimming pool

Alma mater, Altgeld Hall

The Alma mater statue is like the mother of a university and is also a place to take pictures before graduation. The university implies that it is the place where intellectual nourishment is absorbed, and internal growth is achieved before entering a harsh society. From the back, you can see the oldest building in the school, the Altgeld Hall. It is now used as the mathematics department building, and a post office is located inside. I remember searching through Google Maps to buy stamps. I didn't think

Alma mater and Altgeld Hall

there was a school post office in this ancient building.

Hallene Gateway

The gateway was initially created in 1871 and was the entrance to the University Hall, the school's first classroom building. It is the nature of the portal to go to school. However, in 1938, when the classroom ceiling collapsed, the gateway was removed and kept in the architecture department, and eventually moved to Allerton Park, a school-owned park in Monticello.

For some time, its presence was forgotten, but it happened in

Hallene Gateway

1994 to find itself buried under Allerton Park and was rebuilt here in 1998 with the help and donations of the Hallene couple, who graduated in 1951. It is constructed in the form of a plaza, including a fountain pond and a rest area.

Main Quad

The main quad corresponding to the central square of the school was created in 1905. In the 1960s and 1970s, there was a space for free discussion and speech against the Clabaugh Act, which was politically suppressed by even the freedom of school during the Cold War. It was demolished in the early 1990s and now only has traces of red brick floors.

Main Quad (smilepolitely.com)

Morrow Plots

It is the first experimental agricultural research facility in the United States and followed the name of the professor who did the research. It is in the center of the school. It looks like a common cornfield in Illinois, but it was an innovative research facility at that time it was built and was quite large. Of the 90,000 national registered historic sites, only 2,500 are designated as 'National Historic Landmarks' such as Morrow Plots. I've heard of the saying expulsion if breaking in here without permission and eating corn, which seems to be a cyst.

Round Barns

Round Barn is the U.S. National Register of Historic Places, which is a total of three round-shaped granaries. It was built experimentally at the University of Illinois in 1907-1913. It was essentially an indispensable building in the American countryside, not only in the grain but also in the captivity of livestock.

Round barns

It greatly reduced timber than traditional rectangular warehouses, making it more economical to feed animals in a circular way, and especially able to withstand strong winds and tornadoes in the United States. This economic efficiency spread widely to the Midwest, but now there are no more than 60 such round-shaped barns left in the United States.

Memorial Stadium

I've been watching the players' public practice at Zuppke Field in Memorial Stadium, a football stadium at the University of Illinois. Although it was open practice, there were referees. Players in groups were playing it like a regular game. People watched the game with a glass of beer. The opening of the college football

Football stadium, Zuppke Field

league is in September, and public practice will be held once a month from May.

Willard Airport

Only two of the commercial airports in the United States are owned by educational institutions, one of which is Willard Airport. It was created in 1946 and named after the former president of the University of Illinois. It is located in Savoy, south of Champaign.

Currently, American Airlines and United Airlines are flying from and to Chicago's O'Hare Airport and Dallas' Fort Worth Airport, with seven one-way Chicago flights a day and two Dallas flights a day. I also came to Willard Airport from Dallas when I arrived at the Urbana-Champaign. Meanwhile, the trip to the eastern part of the U.S. is likely to be a little more convenient as one flight daily will be added to Charlotte Douglas Airport from December 2018. Airport parking fee is $7 a day, and up to two hours is free.

UIUC golf course

An orange course was created in the 1950s and a blue course in the 1960s. As of the weekday of 2018, the cost of 18 holes is $18 on oranges and $15 on blue for students and $22 and $19, respectively for ordinary people. On weekends, it is about two or three dollars more expensive.

Aside from the 18-hole golf course, there is a golf training center near the school. There are indoor and outdoor training grounds, respectively, and it seems like players on the men's and women's golf teams at the school are training here.

Lincoln Square, Urbana Library

Urbana Farmer's Market is a five-hour market place every Saturday morning, 7:00-12:00 a.m., from early May to early November. A few days ago, I stopped by Monticello's Farmer's Market on my way back from Springfield, but it was too small.

In Urbana Market, there are plenty of food trucks to satisfy your hunger. Among them, the Thai food truck was palatable to us — egg roll, Patai, etc. There were musical performers in the market, and they were exciting people and taking tips.

On that day, my wife and Taeju participated in Ben's Bell Project at Urbana Library. It's a project to make a ceramic hanging wind chime with clay, bells, and strings. It takes time to bake clay, so what we made was completed in the next time and handed over to another person, and we were handed over what was created by another person in the previous time.

I liked the purpose of the project. The story is that such intentional small kindness changes Illinois and the world. No word in English corresponds to 'Jeong' in Korean, but the idea is that such a small kindness is closer to what Americans think of as 'Jeong.'

The bell handed over is hung on my house's fire extinguisher. Taeju made a fish-shaped ceramic with her mom, and she kept asking where it went, so I told her it would be relayed to someone else.

Art project at Urbana Library

[2] Chicago

I left Urbana at 6 a.m. for a daily trip to Chicago with my parents and parents-in-law. I booked a tour through a Chicago travel agency. It was also acting as an agent for Asiana Airlines shuttle service from Chicago O'Hare Airport to three cities, where the University of Illinois, Purdue University and the University of Wisconsin are located.

Coincidentally, the tour guide was my military colleague. Hongcheon, Gangwon Province, 3rd Armored Brigade 56th War Battalion. It was 20 years ago, but my platoon was a little special at the time, and this guy remembered me because I played a lot of soccer with the troops. Then a new 4.2-inch mortar squad with armored vehicles was established in the tank battalion, and I was transferred from Hwacheon with my entire platoon. It is the only new mortar platoon in the tank battalion, and I was the platoon leader.

This guy was a tank pilot and transferred to another unit six months before his discharge. He came to the U.S. in 2000 after being discharged from the military in 1999, and now his travel agency is run by his wife's family, so he is involved together. He has been familiar with this job enough to drive through downtown Chicago in a hand while doing tour broadcasting. I think he is likely to impress traveling customers with his common touch.

The etymology of Chicago is wild onions, a French-type English word for the 'Shikaakwa' spoken by American natives. It was a favorite vegetable of the American natives, and it was popular in this area. In the late 17th century, the French explored through the Mississippi River, and with the help of natives, they learned of the Illinois River, and the Chicago route, which was close to the northern Canadian region where France was based.

Currently, Chicago is one of the top three cities in the U.S. with a population of about 2.5 million, about a quarter of the people of Seoul. Illinois has about 13 million people, and about the same size as South Korea but a quarter of the people.

As we drove through the University of Chicago via the Obama mansion, I heard a brief explanation. Obama, whose daughter is a high school student, is currently in Washington, D.C., and is more likely to return to the Chicago mansion when she enters college. But for security reasons, a tall tree was planted to the fence, so little could be seen.

The University of Chicago is a world-class private university, especially in economics. Its campus was beautiful, and there were many cars parked as it has a quarter-based system, so the school schedule is currently underway in June. Accidents also happen frequently, since the University of Chicago is located in the southern Chicago, while Northwestern University, another prestigious university nearby, located in Evanston, northern Chicago.

Chicago Shore Line

There are three words that I heard the most through the guide and cruise ship announcement. It is the Great Fire, the Chicago Plan, and the World's Fair, which was held twice in Chicago. I took pictures

Chicago shore line as a backdrop

against the backdrop of Chicago shoreline, which was well-ordered and beautifully designed by the Chicago Plan after the Great Fire.

Chicago is a crucial point of railway and waterway transportation due to its geographical location and has grown up rapidly since the Civil War (1861-1865), and it was destroyed mostly by the Great Fire in October 1871. The cause of the fire is unknown, but the fire, which began in a barn west of Chicago, spread over the Chicago River to the east in strong winds and timber buildings, it said. Three hundred people were killed, 100,000 homeless, and many businesses destroyed.

Since then, immigrants from around the world have built new homes and launched businesses, and famous architects have built skyscrapers in an orderly fashion under the Chicago Plan to flourish the industry further. It was the Chicago World Expo 1893 to commemorate the 400th anniversary of Columbus' voyage to the Americas that brought Chicago back to life.

Art Institute of Chicago

If there is a Louvre Museum in Paris, there is the Art Institute of Chicago. Robert Allerton, who donated Allerton Park to the University of Illinois, contributed much to the establishment and operation of the Art Institute of Chicago. So, the main building where major paintings are currently on display is called the Allerton Building. The street ahead is Michigan Avenue, the

The art of Institute of Chicago and Michigan Avenue

main street of Chicago.

Taye's favorite police car and dump truck were parked in front of the museum at the same time. That modern building is Modern Wing, which can be directly crossed to the Millennium Park through a bridge on the roof.

Impressionist collections are representative of painting works, with many people watching arts by Vincent van Gogh, Claude Monet, and Georges Seurat.

I appreciated the work of French post-impressionist artist, Seurat. It features people spending a leisurely Sunday afternoon on the French suburb of Grande Jatte, and I could read a man's expression of hellishness after coming to work Monday and living another week. It is said to be about 3 meters * 2 meters in size, which was much bigger than I thought, and he did preliminary sketches and drawing dozens of times. There was a cafeteria in the basement of the museum, where you could eat hamburgers and hot dogs with drinks.

'A Sunday afternoon on the Island of La Grande Jatte' by Seurat

Millennium Park

It was supposed to open in 2000 to match the name Millennium Park but was completed in 2004 due to delays in construction. It is regarded as one of the greatest achievements in Chicago's history, with a track down and a harmonized layout of sculptures and park facilities designed by world-class architects. It's close to Michigan Avenue, a busy shopping street in Chicago, so it's good to walk.

Cloud Gate is a work that has no joints on the steel plate, giving the exterior and interior a mysterious look like a large mirror. It was designed by Spanish artist Jaume Plensa and is also the most famous piece in the park with his designed Crown Fountain.

Cloud Gate, also known as 'Jelly Bean'

The Crown Fountain comes as the faces of 1,000 Chicago citizens turn around on a 15-meter LED pillar set on both sides. And the facial expression keeps changing, and at one point it spills a fresh column of water out of its mouth. He or she has a smile on the face after pouring water.

Crown Fountain that spills water on Taeju

Designed by architect Frank Gehry and named after Jay Pritzker, a Chicago-born architectural lover,

Jay Pritzker Pavilion. Jay Pritzker is the founder of the Hyatt Hotel, who created the Pritzker Prize, dubbed the Nobel Prize in architecture, and Frank Gehry is also the 1989 winner of the award. Frankly, I don't know the design but I was glad to have a bathroom on both sides of the basement in the concert hall. There seem to be no restrooms in the park other than here.

Outdoor auditorium, Jay Pritzker Pavilion

Wendella Boat Cruise

Thanks to the Great Fire, Chicago has become a world-famous building city, and the best way to appreciate it is through cruise ship architecture tours. First, from the dock, go along the Chicago River toward Lake Michigan, and take the building once. And it was a relatively well-organized curriculum that allowed us to go out of Lake Michigan and look at the buildings again from afar and review them as we entered the dock.

The total tour time is 90 minutes, about 20 minutes of which is used to level the water by filling the floodgates with doors to get out of Lake Michigan. The Chicago River is about two feet below Lake Michigan. In the late 19th century, the Chicago River, polluted by rapid industrialization, dug its bottom to prevent it from flowing into Lake Michigan, a drinking water source for citizens, it said. Instead, they connected it to the Illinois River through the canal and eventually turned the waterways to the Mississippi River. That is what happened in 1900.

Wendella Cruise open seat on the 2nd floor

The American guide in front of the ship memorizes the history of the building and explains it nonstop, but it is not easy to understand fast English, so you need to know the rough details in advance.

The double antennae building on the left is the Willis Tower, the tallest building in Chicago. It is 110 stories high and was built in 1974, the same age as me. It was the tallest building in the world until the 1970s. The building on the right side of the yellow crane is the CBOT (Chicago Board of Trade), one of the two largest futures exchanges in the United States along with the CME (Chicago Mercantile Exchange). At the top of the CBOT stands a 4-ton aluminum statue, named Demeter, the goddess of grain and harvest. The U.S. Midwest is the main production sites of grain, indicating that the main targets of futures trading were also grains. CBOT was merged into CME in 2007 and became a CME Group.

The second-highest building in Chicago is the Trump Tower, built in 2009. The Renaissance building with a clock tower next to its right is Wrigley's building, which is famous for its chewing gum. And the building next to the right is the Gothic Tribune Tower, the headquarters of the Chicago Tribune newspaper.

Behind them are skyscrapers of Chicago, and in front of them is Monroe Harbor, where many ships are moored, including yachts. Lake Michigan is about half the size of South Korea, and seagulls fly around, which are actually like the sea.

Sight of the buildings from Lake Michigan

Chicago revisited

After graduation, I went to Chicago again with my wife and children. It's two and a half hours' drive from Urbana-Champaign, so the weather is almost the same as where we live. Warm weather does not begin until early May in the U.S. Midwest. This day, the sun was hot, but when we entered the shade, it was still chilly.

In general, Chicago tour begins at the museum campus of which houses a planetarium, an aquarium and a museum of natural history. There are many places to park on either side of the bridge, and the price is low at $2 an hour. And most of all, the view was excellent, so we parked there and took it as a starting point for tourism.

The Crown Fountain is also a favorite meeting place for Chicago citizens. On the first day of our visit, we opened our camping gear and watched the screen comfortably because

Camping in the Crown Fountain

it didn't soak water. On the second day, Taeju and Taye loved running around in the water. Children like to play in water fountains in summer without needing anything else.

Buckingham Fountain is located widely in the center of Grant Park, and it has a comprehensive view all around it, which is suitable for viewing buildings. Buckingham Fountain is said to have been the largest fountain in the world until recently, but rather than its size, the atmosphere seems to have come to the Versailles Palace in Paris. Maybe it benchmarked Versailles, so there's a rose garden at the upper side.

There are two zoos in Chicago, a vast Brookfield Zoo in the west of Chicago and a small Lincoln Park Zoo in the north of town. We went to Lincoln Park Zoo recommended by Clint and Chris from Savoy church. Lincoln Park Zoo has a parking fee of $25 instead of no admission fee. I tried to park on the street nearby, but there was already full. Even when a car pulled out, another car was stopped to get in. City life everywhere is hell because of parking. On weekends, it is wise to pay a parking fee in the zoo's parking lot from the start.

Since we were in Chicago, we wanted to try a Chicago pizza. I heard Lou Malnati's is excellent, so googled where it was. We found a store in Wrightwood, 10 minutes northwest of Lincoln Park Zoo. Koreans like thin pizza. I heard that thick deep-dish pizza tasted not so good, but it was very delicious for me. The medium size is about $18, including taxes, and it takes time to cook so that you can pick it up in 30 minutes.

Lincoln Park Zoo: A lion that takes a nap

[3] Springfield

Springfield, Illinois

Springfield is the city of Lincoln and the capital of Illinois. It connects to the Illinois River through the Sangamon River. Illinois became the 21st U.S. state in 1818, and the state capital was Kaskaskia in the south and later changed to Vandalia in 1820 before Springfield began its role in 1839. Springfield is said to be geographically located in the center of the state and was elected by vote.

There is no entrance fee for Lincoln's Home, and the parking fee is $2 an hour. To participate in the guided tour, you must get a ticket from the visitor center. The time to wait was not long because there were many tours.

Lincoln's bedroom

The current State Capitol is a new building built in 1888. It is said that the gray dome stands out from afar and is taller than the Capitol in Washington, D.C. We went to the old Capitol, which was used at the time of Lincoln's activities, and it had a red dome. Obama, who wanted to inherit Lincoln's spirit, announced his declaration of presidential candidacy here in February 2007, beating his political hometown of Chicago.

The picture behind the President of Senate is General Lafayette of France, who made a significant contribution during the U.S. war of Independence. It is said to be a copycat of the federal

Capitol in Washington. General Lafayette plays a crucial role in uniting with the independence forces of General Washington in the battle of Yorktown to lead to the surrender of British troops.

My father becoming the President of Senate

Similarly, like the Federal House, a portrait of a Washington general hangs in the House. Lincoln never had a state senator and was mainly active in the House of Representatives. When Lincoln was assassinated in 1865, his body was brought back here and buried in the tomb, friends and neighbors greeted him lastly in this room.

House of Representatives

Lincoln’s Tomb

Lincoln is said to be buried underground three meters below the stone. There are graves of his wife, Mary Lincoln, and three sons except for one of his four sons, who was a soldier. In other words, it is a family grave.

There is a statue of Lincoln saying that if you touch his nose right in front of the tomb, you will be lucky. They have also prepared a stepping wood to feel it. I also touched it and prayed for good luck in the future.

Lincoln's tomb is located in Oak Ridge Cemetery, where the graves of World War II, Korean War and Vietnam War veterans from Illinois are also located.

Inside of the Lincoln Tomb

LINCOLN

[4] Peoria, Monticello, Decatur

Peoria

Peoria is the name of the indigenous tribe in the region and is also the first European settlement in Illinois. Close to the Illinois River and lakes, American natives have lived for thousands of years and are still an excellent place to fish and hunt. Both agriculture and industry developed. Initially, it was the second largest city in Illinois after Chicago, but its ranking was pushed back by the growing population of satellite cities around Chicago.

The Riverfront area is a major tourist destination for Peoria, and festivals and concerts are also often held. From the end of May to the end of September, the Farmer's Market is held every Saturday morning.

Peoria Riverfront region

There are many main attractions across the way from the cruiser — the civic center, Riverfront Museum, Caterpillar visitor center, etc.

Peoria is home to the headquarters of Caterpillar Inc., a global heavy equipment maker such as bulldozers, dump trucks, and tractors. We visited the head office building beside the lake and looked at souvenir shops. Taye's maternal grandmother bought him a dump truck at the Caterpillar store.

Tickets for Peoria Cruise are sold from 1 p.m. to 1:30 p.m. and Cruise hour is from 2 p.m. to 3:30 p.m. The price is eighteen dollars for adults. What's unique about this ship is that it imitates an old steamboat and moves a large mill around the back. The vessel was antique and gorgeous, but the problem is there was not much to see. There were no buildings around like the Chicago architecture tour, and the riverside was just grassland as it was hundreds of years ago.

We picked the basic 90-minute cruise, besides there was one day, three days, and five days cruise. Some ships travel along the Illinois and Mississippi Rivers to St. Louis, the gateway to the American West, and some to Hannibal, the hometown of Mark Twain, for five days. One ship goes up the Illinois River to Starved Rock, a 40-meter cliff named after a former Illinois tribe surrounded here by another tribe and starved to death.

90-minute Peoria Cruise

Monticello and Decatur

Decatur is a small town of about 80,000 people, located halfway between Champaign and Springfield. It's an hour's drive from Champaign and halfway through Monticello. Allerton Park was in Monticello, so I stopped by first. Geographically, the Sangamon River, which flows through Allerton Park, passes the Decatur to Springfield, meets with the Illinois River, and eventually joins the Mississippi River.

Mainly grown in the Midwest of the United States are corn and soybeans, where the Decatur is called the Soybean City, the home of soybeans. Champaign County produces the most soybeans in the U.S. and corn is first in nearby McLean County.

Allerton Park is a park and resort in Monticello, owned by the University of Illinois. It's about 40 minutes' drive from Champaign. Robert Allerton, the son of the founder of the First National Bank of Chicago, has been especially fond of art since he was a child and has collected many sculptures while traveling around the world. He has been living in Allerton Park by decorating the collection and making gardens. He had various exchanges with the nearby University of Illinois and eventually donated the entire park to the university in 1946.

Allerton Park guided tour program

My family took part in the garden tour in Allerton Park on Saturday, July 21. Allerton Park has 14 gardens in total, and a free guided tour is held once a month. (May to October, third Saturday of every month)

The above garden is called 'Brick wall Garden,' and the sculpture's name is 'Girl with a Scarf.'

Located on the crossroad in the middle of the garden is a copy of Rodin's sculpture, 'Adam.' It was Rodin's sculpture of the first human Adam. Rodin was fascinated by Michelangelo while traveling in Italy, and 'Adam' was also much inspired by Michelangelo's work.

Avenue of the Chinese Musicians

Sunken Garden is a must-see. Fish-shaped sculptures surround them, making children busy riding. Another statue and the street are called 'Avenue of the Chinese Musicians.'

In Decatur, we visited Scovill Zoo. Four members of my family paid 22 dollars to enter. Taeju had gone to the zoo by school bus from the school summer camp. She ran off to get in, as she had a good memory then.

What's special about the Scovill Zoo is that it has room to feed the goats and to touch them to their heart's content. There is also space where you can wash your hands after touching them. There were many goats full of pregnancy. It was clear to me that the primary job of animals was to eat, sleep, and make babies. Goat, unable to produce its young, is like losing its role in the world of goats. It is different from the human world.

A place where you can feel the goat

My children liked Guinea pigs the

most because they were cute. Also, we met with two-toed sloths. My wife is watching in close as if she has met her same species.

Taeju's ability to cross the monkey bar has improved a lot. She used to play at the Orchard Downs Community Center playground, and she could easily pass that four times today.

Crossing monkey bar

There is a famous hamburger shop, Krekel's Custody in Decatur. I heard that some people come to visit on purpose from afar. Krekel's here is carry-out food and had a few tables at the back of the parking lot. But while we were eating there, our family was severely beaten by striped mosquitoes. Mosquitoes are too many and bite to be very strong.

We also visited Millikin University in Decatur. There's a statue of Lincoln in front of the university. The phrase says that at the age of 21, Lincoln first came here to build a log cabin in Macon County, Illinois, and that's his first home in Illinois. Macon County is an area that includes Decatur and is connected to Springfield via the Sangamon River. I first came to Illinois at the age of 44 and haven't had my home yet.

Lincoln's mother, Nancy Lincoln (1784-1817), died when he was eight years old by Milk sickness from a cow that ate a poisonous grass. Lincoln's family left Indiana, where the Milk sickness was spreading when he was 21 years old and moved near the Decatur, Illinois. Lincoln came down the river by canoe to the village of New Salem. Lincoln is said to have been working as a boatload of goods to the south of New Orleans on the Sangamon and Mississippi rivers.

He lost his first political election to the Illinois legislature in 1832, studied law on his own, and was certified as a lawyer in 1833. Starting with the election of the U.S. Congress in 1834, he was defeated in the federal senator's election twice and finally won the 16th U.S. presidency in 1860.

Lincoln's statue at Millikin University

3.3 Summer Life

Fish-like swimming

Total Immersion (TI) is a training method for swimming without effort like a fish created by Terry Laughlin. Usually, the swimming we do is a quick way to stir using our hands and feet. On the other hand, TI swimming is a way to swim by weight shift using the entire body, so that we can swim long, easy, and not tired, but rather fast.

Terry Laughlin, Who Taught Swimmers Not to Struggle, Dies at 66

Terry Laughlin demonstrating the crawl stroke at his pool in New Paltz, N.Y., in 2013. Robert Fagan

By Daniel E. Slotnik

Oct. 27, 2017

Terry Laughlin, who developed a popular method of swimming instruction that emphasized form over speed to help thrashing swimmers learn to glide through the water, died on Oct. 20 in Albany. He was 66.

According to my experience, the key to this swimming method is to slide forward while still putting your weight toward your head. The biggest reason why it's hard to swim comfortably is that your butt sink as your weight falls back. The buoyancy of the body in the water is in both lungs, so keep tilting toward the head so you can swim with your heavy buttocks and the center of gravity.

The problem is that when you breathe, your balance often collapses as you lift your head, but the TI swimming method tells you to breathe through the body's left and right roll. Instead of raising your head to breathe, breathe in on your side for a while, using the natural turn in the process of moving forward. Breathing on both sides is useful in aspects of swimming balance, but in my case, I am not familiar with the left side.

Unfortunately, I remember reading Terry Laughlin's obituary in the New York Times last year. He was 66 years old, and according to her daughter, prostate cancer was the cause. The title of the article, "He taught swimmer not to struggle" is impressive. The main point of his teaching is not to struggle in the water but to glide. Unlike air, water is so resistant that even if you try to fight it, it will not speed up and will lose strength only.

Lawn mower and John Deere

In the U.S., people with houses are routinely mowing lawns in their spare time, and some even travel across the continent on lawn mower. Because there is a lot of green space in my graduate family housing, lawn mower tractors often turn around a few times a week in summer.

The problem is that the machine is so loud and annoying that I'd rather leave the grass alone. But it is true that it is hard to walk if the grass is too long. There are many times to walk on the grass here. Instead, we need a machine that can mow the lawn quietly. That green little John Deere machine is louder than the armored vehicle I used to ride in the army. It makes a high-pitched squeal, not a heavy, low-pitched sound.

John Deere lawn mower

John Deere is the

founder and company name of the world's leading agricultural machinery maker, which began in Illinois. The company's motto is "Nothing runs like a Deere." It symbolically uses green and yellow and the name Deere is the same pronunciation as deer. It produces not only various farming tools such as tractors but also lawnmower and massive equipment engines.

Until the 1700s, the land in the Midwest was covered with low bushes called prairie. Because it was swamped millions of years ago, trees all died and became fertile soil on the ground, and the earth became as flat as it is now while glaciers repeatedly came and stepped down. Since then, in this fertile, flat land, where trees have died and disappeared, the prairie has flourished.

In the 1800s, Europeans moved to live and began farming. Prairie had beautiful flowers and trees, but the roots were strong and deep, so it was hard to remove them. Some say the roots stretch 4-5 meters below the ground. In 1838, John Deere invented the steel plow, not the traditional cast iron, to dramatically help farm the tough prairie roots. It's the hard-earned removal of prairie, but ironically, there's a movement in the 21st century to restore prairie, which has been on the ground for thousands of years, all over the place.

Fourth of July, Independence Day of the U.S.

The Independence Day of the United States is July 4, 1776, when Thomas Jefferson made the Declaration of Independence and was approved by Congress, not 1783 when it gained independence from Britain after eight years of war. The core point of the Declaration of Independence is that individuals have the gift of God and the state has no right to hurt it, and if they violate it, the people can abolish the government and establish a new government to protect their rights.

> "We hold these truths to be self-evident, that all men are created equal, that they are endowed by their Creator with certain unalienable Rights, that among these are Life, Liberty and the pursuit of Happiness."

Independence Day was a big celebration in the United States. About 130 teams held a parade in the morning, concert events in the afternoon and fireworks were held in the evening. Therefore, according to the TV series Forensic Files, there are many crimes that occurred on Independence Day.

The parade runs along the street, and we watched near the starting place of the show. When we had just arrived, the Taekwondo team was passing by.

The parade was attended by many nearby high school marching bands and was the most spectacular. One school marched with a big frog balloon in front, but frogs should have kept blowing air in the back, fearing a fall in the wind, and several people pulled strings around, creating a rare scene. There were also many parades with large trailer commonly seen on highways in the U.S.

Those who marched also carried a whole bunch of candy and chocolate and sprinkled mercilessly on the spectators. Thanks to this, we received more than one

High school marching band with large frog

bottle, and my children and wife filled their stomach with sweets so that we didn't have to eat lunch.

We had a concert from 7 p.m., and although the lawn was shaded, it was so hot that we took refuge at the mart. Furthermore, the grass was more uncomfortable because of the humidity.

We stopped by Meijer for Independence Day shopping and happened to buy two camping chairs for $12. Americans usually sit on the front porch of their homes and carry camping chairs during outdoor camping and other events, which is almost a necessity.

On the second floor of the State Farm Center, we put a camping chair and watched the fireworks in a comfortable position, and it was very lively to see them right around the corner. At the Yeouido Fireworks Festival in Korea, it is unimaginable because of the crowds. They shot the fireworks nonstop for half an hour. It was the best fireworks in my life. The way out was a bit stuck, but it was a good day.

Fireworks in Urbana-Champaign

Quiet time between Taye and wife

Since Taye is 2.5 years old, he still needs a lot of affection from his mom, but my wife sometimes gets tired. The best way to help them is to keep them apart for a while when Taye keeps pushing his mom around the kitchen. I step in only when I don't think my wife can do it herself.

Struggle between wife and Taye

I take Taye to his room and tell him to stay away for a while. I explain that you should not be so noisy. Then take a quiet time to reflect on himself in the room for 10 minutes. I think this is better. Last year I locked the door outside so that I wouldn't let him out, then he knocked on the door and cried out loud to get out.

This time, he doesn't come out of the room without locking the door, but he stays in the place. He feels free from anxiety because the door is open, and he lies down quietly by himself. Sometimes I sit in the room near him and read books while he is punished. After a while, everyone feels much better.

Firefly

Many fireflies fly in the arboretum in front of my house or the grass behind the house. Bright lights flash when viewed late in the afternoon or at night, just like LED lights. It is good to hear that fireflies only live in places where the natural environment is clean. It's a great night to see Taeju and her downstairs friend, Angel running for fireflies.

Birthday Bingo and coloring book

The Orchard Downs Community Center holds an event called Birthday Bingo every month. It's not about giving presents to a birthday person that month, but about getting together and playing bingo games and giving gifts to a winner. Taeju was upset because she didn't win every time, but this time, Taeju and her mom won a coloring book and a cup with the red light as a prize. Taeju's birthday is March, and it's not even a few months old, but she's already waiting for her birthday to come soon.

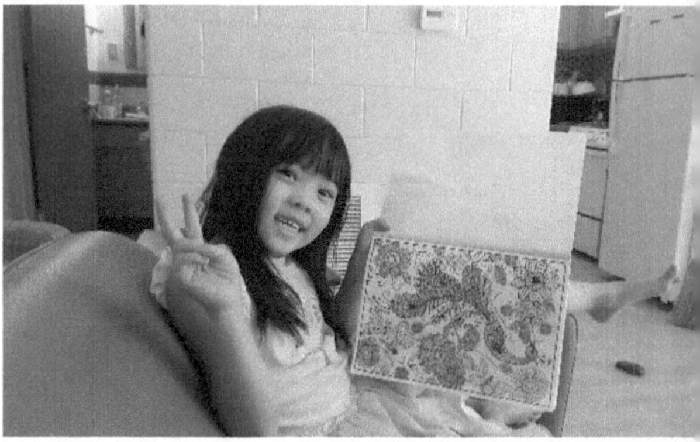
Coloring book gift at Birthday Bingo

'Progressive' car insurance

It's good to switch to direct online insurance because the price is lower, and counseling is available through online chatting. You can also receive additional discounts through a device called Snapshot when you sign up for the first time. The Snapshot system monitors my driving record for six months by plugging it under the driver's seat and calculates accident-prone probability based on driving habits to

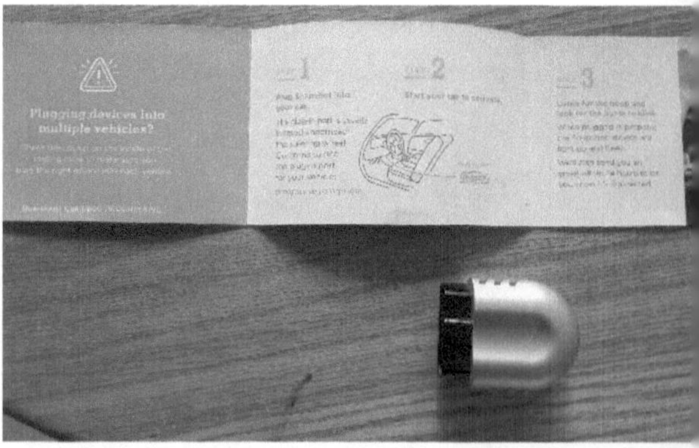
Snapshot device of Progressive car insurance

discount/increase insurance premiums. I paid about $360 in insurance for six months, but when I completed the Snapshot, I got a $40 discount from next time.

However, I was surprised that the next six months' premiums were up slightly to $370. It is said that the discount on the eSign contract is about $60 for first-time subscribers, but not for the next one. The reason has been confirmed, but the strategy seems to be to attract a large number of customers at first. That is, once they become customers, they will not choose to move in the next contract unless there is a significant issue.

I finally renewed my six-month contract with the same coverage. 'Bodily Injury & Property Damage Liability,' which is a liability insurance policy, has chosen to cover $50,000 per person and $100,000 per case. 'Collision or Comprehensive' that are eligible for self-insurance were excluded. So, if I drive in the West and run into a deer, I have to fix my car with my own money. Only 'Bodily Injury' was covered except for 'Property' in case of negligence of the other 'Uninsured or Underinsured Motorist.' 'Roadside Assistance' is essential when oil runs out on the highway or needs for towing, so it's worth about ten dollars. The 'Medical Payment' item is no-fault coverage, which is paid regardless of whether or not it is your negligence and has only been secured at the $1,000 limit.

Apart from auto insurance, license plate registration costs are also required to be paid every year. If you spend $101 online, you'll get a sticker by mail in 5-10 days. It's a very primitive way to attach the label to one side of the license plate.

Mathematics study

Financial engineering is an area that optimizes financial practice by implementing financial mathematics theory through computer programming, so the mathematical foundation is essential. I am reviewing math during summer break using a textbook for the GRE Mathematics Subject Test, which is the best book I have ever read.

Compared to the hard-written proof-oriented math books in college, the basic concepts of college mathematics are easily, and lucidly well organized. Practice problems are also useful. Looking at the author's bibliography later, Steven Leduc graduated from MIT and has devoted his entire life to math and physics education. If I want to write a book that is good for the world, I will have to write one like this book.

Fire alarm

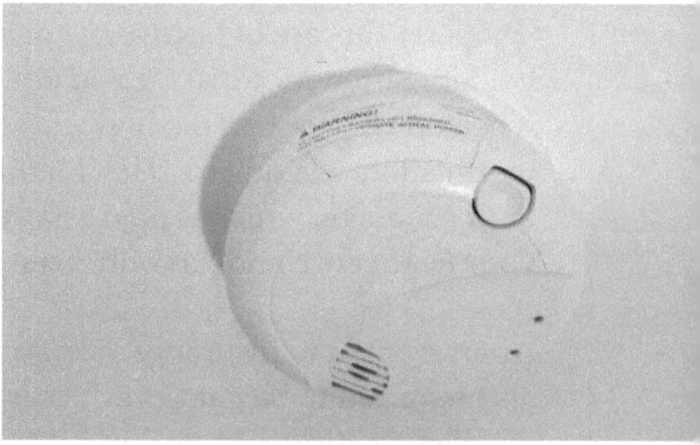

Fire detector on ceiling

A few days ago, a fire alarm suddenly went off at home. My wife said that her cooking of kimchi pancakes seemed to be the cause of the signal. But it seems to be out of order because it rang twice more at night. The four fire alarms are ringing at the same time, and the sound is so loud and annoying that I can't do anything until I turn it off. It's supposed to work for eight minutes once it starts.

I urgently contacted the housing office night shift, and he replaced some of them. The funny thing was that it sounded once when he was around, but he took off his hat and fanned it right under the detector, and it stopped. I don't know the mechanism, but it seems to be designed to prevent sensors when they are fanned.

Summer camp for children

Children's summer camp is being held for a week at the Orchard Downs Community Center. Since TCBC church organizes the camp, children also seem to be asked to memorize some Bible passages.

Taeju has never memorized a Bible phrase, but on the first day and the second day, teachers gave candy as a prize to a person who memorized well. She kept muttering something afterward. I heard she grabbed two teachers and memorized them today. Taeju asked why they didn't give him candy. Finally, today, Taeju ate candy. The phrase is John 14:6.

> Jesus answered, "I am the way and the truth and the life. No one comes to the Father except through me."

For one thing, Taeju used to pronounce Jesus as [Jises] for a long time, but she's stubborn even if I try to fix it today. "You'll do what you want. I'll do what I want to do." Pronunciation is a kind of social promise. Does it make sense to do what she wants to do?

Hawaii bicycle trip two years ago

Not long ago, there was a volcanic eruption in Hawaii. Mt. Kilauea in Big Island, which is part of Volcano National Park

North coast of Oahu, Hawaii

in Hawaii. When I visited there in 2016, it was only farting, but this time I think it got a little poop.

It reminded me of Hawaii again when I saw a panoramic photo created by artificial intelligence on Google Photos. That is where I took a rest while riding a bicycle through the northern beach. The wave of north shores is so high in winter that they become a heaven for surfing. At that time, the waves were considerable though it was early November.

What I felt while cycling around the island of Oahu in Hawaii for a few days is that the United States is not the right country to travel long distances by bicycle. First of all, the design of the road itself is car-centric, so there are few bike paths other than the city, which is too dangerous and bothers the car a lot. There are also many large trucks transporting goods across the vast continent, and when such a large vehicle passes, the bicycle is staggering.

It's pitch-dark darkness outside the town, with no lights at all, scary when the sun sets and no one you can ask for help. The idea that the U.S. is not suitable for bicycle travel compared to Europe has become more concrete after car trips to the West.

Last year, my bicycle that was loaded into an airplane and brought hard from Korea was resting at home. For here, the winter weather is long and cold to commute to school by bicycle as the bus is convenient to go to school. And the danger of the theft is so high that everyone locks their bikes with a steel U-lock that looks so awful.

My road bike and bike trailer

These days, however, as I reread the <American Bicycle Tour> after a few years, I feel the desire for a bicycle wriggle. While I was thinking about it, I went to the mart to get a cheap bike lock. The password is 'HOOK' set in the factory.

And I retook the road bike this morning, which I left inside the house. It is a model called KHS Flite 500 ten years ago; also named Ku Hye-Sun or Kim Hye-Soo after the brand's initials.

I used to think that bike riding is not an exercise like jogging. It's been a long time since I've been on the road bike high saddle, and I realized taking a drop-bar posture is a hard exercise in itself.

Taeju's finger addition

Not long ago, I remember my wife wondering that Angel in the lower house is already studying subtraction. Taeju, who is six years old and the same age, is still not well added.

Taeju and Angel in the Community Center

Today, Taeju suddenly put out a 12 + 12 =? quiz, and she thought the answer was 22. When I answered 24, she started counting with her fingers and mouth. She folded her fingers one by one, adding 12 to her mouth, "Thirteen, Fourteen, and ..." But, since she had ten fingers, she had a hard time adding 12. In the end, she could fold two fingers one more time and get the answer 24.

Come to think of it, humans' use of decimals has to do with ten fingers. So, the computer has two fingers? The two-toed sloths in the zoo yesterday also had two fingers and two toes.

Even after that, it is often hard to push dad and mom to give her more question. If parents call a little larger number, she'll be angry to call inside 20. I think she has learned to subtract from school, but it's much slower to calculate than adding.

Urbana shooting

There were two gun-accidents in Urbana last Friday night. One was the murder of a man in his 20s who was shot to death while in a car at an Urbana Townhouse party, and the other was that a teenage boy was shot while riding a bicycle. In particular, the shooting of a teenage boy took place in Beech Street near the King School of Taeju. The safety situation didn't look perfect because it was a black residential area.

The two incidents do not seem to have anything to do with each other, but what they have in common is that they happened around midnight Friday night and fired several shots because of their clear intention to kill. The man in his 20s, believed to be Hispanic black, had a record of transporting heroin, and the fight at the party was the cause of the accident, the newspaper reported.

The U.S. is being massed shot to death, but gun control at the government level is not being done for political reasons. Anyway, if the two incidents are a lesson, then the way to lower the chances of being involved in a gun accident in the United States should never touch drugs and never be around late at night.

Taeju's 2018-19 school registration

In the U.S., parents should register for the next school year of children in unison at the end of July, and the fall semester is the beginning of the school year. The Urbana School District (USD 116) schools are being accepted by Urbana Middle School en masse today.

Urbana School District registration day

There are too many paper documents for the U.S. to write as usual. Each of the more than ten letter pages was read, signed, and submitted with the required information.

Parents' personal information and contact information is basic and there are a number of topics such as who has the authority to pick up children other than parents, how to commute to school, who to do if they can't contact their parents, which hospital they're going to send to during an Emergency, whether they have treatments that parents refuse, whether they can expose them to pictures or interviews, and whether schools can allow the use of the Internet.

I wondered if there was room to store that much information on paper every year, and I wonder if they could find it quickly in an emergency. Of course, unlike Korea, there are not many students in the school, so most teachers can know who she is by the name of Taeju.

While the father was struggling with paperwork, the children were playing in other school's reception area with cute dolls, leaving their school.

A free dental examination

From the Smile Healthy program, children had a free dental checkup at the Orchard Downs Community Center. It is an association of social security dental programs, headquartered in Champaign, where my wife had a broken tooth and got a treatment last time.

Today, Taeju and Taye had fluoride applications. In the case of Taeju, she was consulted about molar permanent teeth sealant. Her mom was worried that Taeju might not be able to sealant because her permanent teeth were going to decay. But the doctor said it was possible for now. Not here today and available at Champaign headquarters or Parkland College.

Taye cried loudly at the medical examiner's office, so someone in the other room wondered what happened to the child. The doctor says Taye has a slight cavity in his front teeth, but he's too young to treat it now. I hardly ever went to the dentist, so I didn't know much, but I feel I need to know basic dental knowledge for my wife and children.

Champaign-Urbana Day

We went to Douglas Park for Champaign-Urbana Day. As the park is located in the north, many black people live in the area. Anyway, I have never seen such an event. I thought I was in Africa. They are all black people except police, three or four white people, and my family.

Even if Obama became president, it's the story of some successful African-American people, and the racial barrier between blacks and whites still seems elusive. It's more accurate to say that people are likely to get along with who are comfortable.

Champaign-Urbana Public Health District

Champaign-Urbana Public Health District is located near Highway 74 north of Champaign. No. 74 is an interstate highway from Indianapolis to Champaign and then to Bloomington and Peoria. It is a local health center for children and pregnant women's health, so there are no general adults.

Champaign-Urbana Day in Douglas Park

Taeju had four molar sealants and received various other checkups. In the end, she also had fluoride applications. The next reservation is in three months. It was lunchtime, so waiting place soon became quiet.

We also received a set of children's toothpaste and toothbrushes. Since brushing is something everyone has to do for life, I feel it is crucial to have a proper brushing habit since we were young. Brushing teeth should be done from the inside where the toothbrush is not easily accessible, and the teeth and gums should feel as if they touch the toothbrush at the same time to remove plaque between the teeth and teeth. Also, toothpaste contains detergents, so after brushing your teeth, you should rinse it with water three times or more. I heard brushing your teeth twice a day and flossing once helps remove plaque between your gums. But I rarely practice it.

Free agricultural products are also being distributed to people there. You can get it every Thursday between 1 and 3 p.m. It has opened space to take potatoes, corn, cherry, and tomatoes from the backyard garden of the health center for free.

Back-to-school night

Taeju will be the first-grade student of King School this fall semester. Elementary schools in the U.S. have a time for parents and their children to visit schools through an event 'Back-to-school

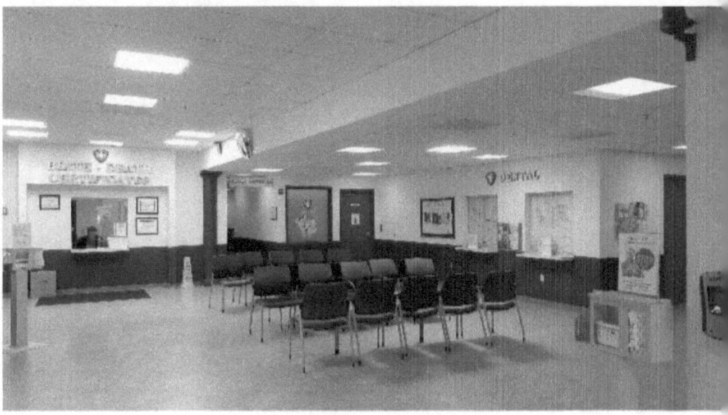

Dental Care waiting place

night' just before the long summer break ends and the school begins. I met Taeju's new homeroom teacher, Mrs. Spencer-Tanner, and got a new school bag and school supplies. We ate hot dogs, snacks, and spent time at the playground.

When Taye is wearing a child harness, he sometimes lies down and tries to hold on. There is no particular home for Taye, and the place where he lies is home.

Princess Jasmine's face occupies the front in the backpack of Taeju. Jasmine is one of the princess series of Disney animations. Press in the middle of the bag, and light comes in on the stick Princess Jasmine has.

New backpack with Princess Jasmine

Part 4. Last Semester (Fall 2018)

In my last semester, I worked hard to bring my entire study to a successful conclusion while organizing what had been taught. I was swamped taking four major courses, including practicum class with Morgan Stanley.

Having lived in the U.S. for a year, I can now roughly understand American life and also university schedule. Overall, I'm happy to graduate safely with about 3.5 out of 4.0 grade. I feel I have to do something worthwhile in the world based on this study, but I'm worried about how to orient myself.

4.1 School: Future of Financial Engineering

Future of Financial Engineering

To gauge the future, we need first to understand the past and the present. Starting with the Black-Scholes equation in the 1970s, finance has gradually become a field of applied mathematics. As mathematics was widely applied to the valuation of financial instruments in the 1980s and 1990s, many Ph.D.s in physics who are good at mathematical and engineering methodologies made inroads into the quant job. And in the 2000s, demand for derivatives grew exponentially, resulting in a shortage of quant workforce. However, the Ph.D. program was so long that many short-term financial engineering programs were made in schools with excellent math and engineering departments.

In other words, it is a one- to two-year fast-track program to get a quant job. While some may have just wanted to study like me, not to find a job, most of the students are looking to earn a higher salary more than investing in tuition by working in the U.S. However, it seems that it is not easy to get a quant job in the U.S. because financial engineering lost its edge due to the 2008 financial crisis and because the U.S. Job market has more supply than demand. Anyway, the majority of students currently in the Financial Engineering program at U.S. universities are mostly from China and India, and some are from the U.S., Korea, Europe, South America, and Africa.

Despite the difficulty of finding a quant job in the U.S., I don't think the future of a master's degree in financial engineering is bad. At present, it is the best way to learn financial engineering properly. Even if you don't get a quant job, it's the easiest way to enter the business street of New York or Chicago. If you prove your ability, you can get the chance you want. And it will be a trend in the future for individuals to learn quantitative investment based on knowledge of financial engineering, as the boundaries of the quant as a profession will become blurred.

Office of Financial Engineering at the University of Illinois

For reference, the University of Illinois has a joint venture program with the Department of Industrial Engineering in the College of Engineering and the Department of Finance in the College of Business. Most other universities are thought to be similar. If you are seriously interested in the UIUC's Financial Engineering program, I recommend you discuss it by email. Writing English e-mail is an essential part of business writing, and as an adult graduate student, you need to practice making a relationship with school staff. Contact to *msfe@illinois.edu*.

No one knows exactly whether it will be promising in the future, so it's better to consider it with reference only. If you find out what you want to do and like it in any field and build your professional skills, you will have to see the light of day. In Marcus Aurelius' <Meditations>, my favorite is the following phrase. (Book4, 31)

"Love the art which you have learnt, and take comfort in it. Go through the remainder of your life in sincere commitment of all your being to the gods, and never making yourself tyrant or slave to any man."

Information about the selection of U.S. school

The U.S. has a different academic schedule system from Korea, with the most representative being the quarter-based and semester-based system. Most universities implement the semester-based system, and only about 20 percent of the central and western regions use the quarter-based system.

Semesters are divided into 'fall semester' in late-August and mid-December, 'spring semester' in early January, and summer break is three and a half months. In comparison, the quarter system or the three-semester system divides the semester into 10-12 weeks, and the school schedule is said to be tight because the summer break is short. The quarter system was first introduced at the University of Chicago in the late 18th century and later at the University of California. A growing number of universities are now returning to the semester system due to the aforementioned side effects.

The other is the choice of school in a college town or large cities. The U.S. has no reason to insist on big cities, as its infrastructure, such as K-12 schools, hospitals, and mart, is all similarly well in rural areas. Some people say they are too bored in a college town, but, during the semester, students are so busy that they don't have enough time to sleep. If you like city life, you can travel and enjoy as much as you like using the long summer break. Especially if you are studying abroad with your family or children, I recommend you choose a college town without fail.

Coursera, MIT Open Course

The content is good, but it does not exactly match to one's purpose, so it is challenging to keep up, and there is no interaction at all. And most of the courses are not free, so people are hesitant in their choices. In the end, it is best to find and refer to videos that are needed through Google search for specific topics. And sometimes excellent courses are caught in Korea's K-MOOC and KOCW while doing a Google search.

Bloomberg terminal

There are about five Bloomberg terminals in my department's computer lab. I hooked up with the team members who were doing the practicum this semester and tried to connect to the terminal. We wanted to check the current prices of five-year and ten-year Treasury Notes. At this purpose, Bloomberg function code BTMM can be used.

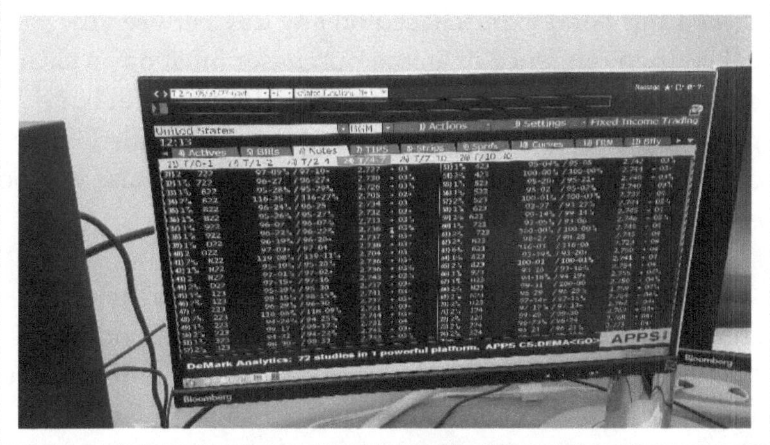

US Treasury Notes at Bloomberg terminal

As it is currently September 2018, the five-year bonds will be due in September 2023. For example, look at data line number 66 on the screen above.

66)	1 3/8	923	93-16	93-16 ¾	2.754	+04

The first field, 1 and 3/8, is the coupon rate, which in turn means 1.375%. U.S. Treasury bonds have a coupon payment cycle of six months or twice a year. The second field 923 shows maturity and is now a five-year bond because it is September 2023. The third field 93-16 is the best bid price, so the highest price people would like to buy. The U.S. bond market uses the 32-base method for decimal points, so is 93+16/32 = 93.5, which means that the best bid price is $935 for bonds with a face value of $1,000. The fourth field is the best ask price, which is not much different from the bid price, so this bond looks very liquid. The fifth field 2.754 is the bond price yield.

Because these are secondary markets in which bonds are circulated, even five-year bonds may have been issued 30 years ago and are now five-year bonds, or seven-year bonds and are now five-year bonds. And it's the 'clean price' of the bond, which is the exact cut price on the basis of the coupon payment date, so if this bond is purchased on any day between the actual coupon reference date, the purchaser must pay a clean price plus the number of days of accrued interest that have elapsed since the last coupon payment date. It is called 'dirty price.' In other words, the actual price on the purchase will be mostly slightly higher than the quoted price.

There are three main methods of day counting for interest calculation: The Treasury Note and the Treasury Bond use actual/365, the Treasury Bill uses actual/360, and the corporate bond generally uses 30/360 methods.

Michael Bloomberg started the business in 1981 when he was fired from Salomon Brothers. And, at present, securities firms around the world are provided all the data they need in practice from Bloomberg terminals, so its market share is overwhelming, unable to work without Bloomberg terminals.

However, there is a joke that it equals with the salary of an assistant manager because it costs almost 30,000 dollars per year to use the line, as the monthly fee is well over 2,000 dollars, and the use of PCs, monitors, and keyboards is also required to rent. Michael Bloomberg is now one of the wealthiest political heavyweights in the world, having been elected to the mayor of New York City twice based on his success in this project and also has a media group on economic broadcasting.

Bloomberg keyboard

Problem using Korean in English Windows 10

1. There was a phenomenon where the file name sent from Korea was shown to be broken even though there was no big problem with installing the Korean input method (IME) provided by Windows itself.
   This problem was solved by changing the settings. (Change the following items to Korean)
   Settings > Time & Language > Region & Language > Administrative language settings > Language for non-unicode programs

2. Another problem is that I could not read Korean properly, which is encoded in UTF-8. A method of using Korean for MS Windows operating system is CP949 that extends the complete form of Hangul (EUC-KR) in MS. However, many servers

usually use the combination form of UTF-8 method, so if I just read it in Windows, the letters look broken.

While writing this book, I used 'Wikidocs,' but while reconfiguring the table of contents, I made the mistake of getting dozens of sub-page erased together. 'Wikidocs' was making daily backups and was able to receive backup files from the administrator, but the problem is all the Korean words seemed to break up.
In the end, the restoration was made by reading and pasting pages in the Korean word processor 'HWP.'

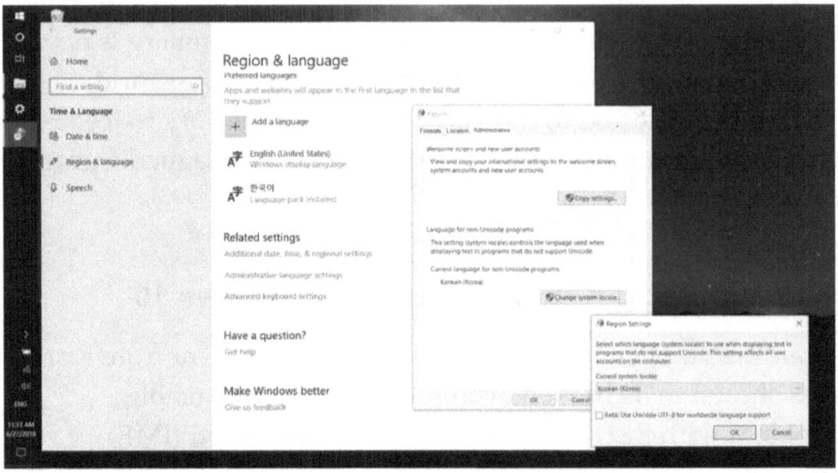

Finding alternatives to Yahoo API service

As Yahoo was sold to Verizon in May 2017, it ended its free API service for the stock price. Since most financial books that were written so far rely on Yahoo APIs, there was a big problem with finding other services to correct the code. The following three alternatives seem likely at present. Three options are EOD historical data, IEX, and Alpha Vantage. But more fundamentally, it is best to build your own databases locally instead of relying solely on real-time APIs.

Fundamentally, it is best to download stock price data from securities firms such as 'Interactive Brokers' and pile it on my master ledger. That is called the 'security master database.' In other words, a personal trading infrastructure system with MySQL and Python is essential for personal research.

Elevator pitch and 3-minute power

There is a saying, elevator pitch, or elevator speech. It refers to the training that makes self-introduction effective in a short time. It is a must-do gateway to get a job in the U.S. It comes from the fact that you have to appeal and make a strong impression in a short time until you get off when you happen to meet a company executive in an elevator.

When I heard about the elevator pitch, I remembered the book called <3-Minute Power> written by Nobuo Takai, which I had read earlier. It's about communication skills learned while working as a lawyer in the human resources/labor field for 40 years. In short, 'three minutes' is the best code to establish relationships in modern society and to make one's perception of one's opponent. It feels like a short time, but, in a busy world, no one listens to me more, and if you don't appeal within three minutes, the other party will be bored already.

Math modeling language, AMPL

I'm going to be crazy because every subject uses a different programming language. So far, the programming languages that I have used to do homework for each subject is C++, Python, R, and Matlab. And AMPL should be added to this.

AMPL is a mathematical modeling language named after the initials of 'A Mathematical Programming Language.' The advantage of AMPL is that notation is similar to actual mathematical expression. Therefore, it is used a lot in the field of optimization.

However, if you want to learn how to use the language and related libraries, you will have to spend a few weeks learning them. In my experience, every programming language does. But, professors encourage students, saying, "It is too easy compared to C, so don't worry." I think the main reason to stick to the various programming language is that the original class materials are written in that language.

Anyway, I'm doing a lot of trial and errors this time while doing my homework using AMPL, and I am even referencing the AMPL tutorial posted by Wong Wang on YouTube. I am also e-mailing the professor and the teaching assistant to ask.

Obama's speech

On September 7, 2018, former U.S. 44th President Barack Obama visited the University of Illinois. It was to win the Douglas Award and give a commemorative lecture. Due to security reasons, participants were limited to students, and about 1,000 students were randomly selected after receiving applications in advance. I applied too but was not chosen, so I had to watch it live on the Internet.

I thought he would talk about his life as a retired president, but I was a little surprised by the strong political rhetoric that was openly swearing at Trump. Oh, yes, it suddenly occurred to me that Obama is a politician. Obama's speech is that, in short, in this November's midterm elections, the Trump administration, which runs counter to the times, must be judged by vote.

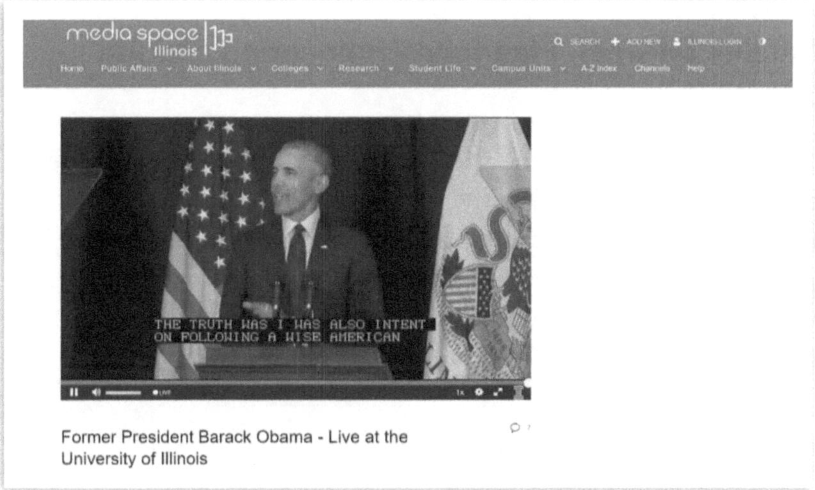

Watching Obama's speech through a video stream

The U.S. midterm elections have the character of a mid-term assessment of the current administration, as it replaces one-third of 100 senators and elects more than 400 new members of Congress. The senator has a six-year term, and the congressman has a two-year term.

Ten hours a day

No matter how smart your brain is, everything will mature over time, and the fruits of your efforts will be made. Time flies by itself, but on the other hand, it's up to you. Time goes slow if you take a slow breath and reflect on it, but when you are impatient with your homework, which is due today, you feel as if time is running faster.

No smart, diligent person will be able to work 20 hours a day. I can concentrate on my work for up to 10 hours a day. It is not desirable to lengthen the time too much. It is also necessary to take a break. In conclusion, how to spend 10 hours a day is the key to our life.

The link between Financial Engineering and life

Learning that is not connected to real life is not fun. And if we study science and engineering only, we can't go beyond the limits of a technician. We need to research based on humanities. It's about the humanities study that writer Lee Ji-sung puts so much emphasis on in <Thinking Humanities>. Find these connections and make them an advantage I can have over the usual young and smart students.

The power of thought

I don't want to study, and I'm exhausted because the midterm exam for my last semester is over. Let's calm down through contemplation. It would be nice if I could take a walk every day at a specific time, like Kant, but of course, there would be no locals who would look at me and set their clocks.

Presentation tips from my experiences

Practicum classes are held in conference calls, so they are slightly different from the usual PowerPoint presentations, but the basic principles of presentation are the same.

1. The presentation material is only a supplement to the presentation. Make the listeners look at me.
2. Emphasize the beginning and the end so that it remains in people's memories.
3. Use one visual for each topic. It's best to remember by image.

Golf & elections lose as soon as you raise your head

Park Jie-won, who is called the ninth-dan politician, often used it in the media. If you raise your head to see whether your ball can go far away after hitting the ball, golf will be ruined due to disorganized posture and lack of follow-throughs, and if a politician is arrogant in the election, he will lose right away. The same goes for studying. If I raise my head that I did well on the midterms, the final exam gets bad, and I lose my grades right away.

10 million dollars in the account

The algorithm trading class ended with the last class today. The professor showed us a screenshot at the end, which is said to be an account with 10 million dollars. I didn't catch the exact explanation, but I guess it's a motivation for students to work hard in this field as the professor has a high-frequency trading major and earned that money.

I am not sure if it's a real account, or if it's a kind of game money. What's clear is that he is a kind, but a peculiar person.

Importance of questioning and answering

According to Dr. Ko Mi-sook's book, <Homo Kungfus>, there is a saying, "If you don't ask questions, you don't exist." Questioning is critical in learning. What I am curious about is that I think about it, and through questions and answers, I become more robust in my knowledge and thoughts.

However, many people find it annoying to be asked, so you need to ask but do well. American professors are okay because they are used to being asked questions, but some classmates don't like to be asked questions. Students from Asia have a stronger tendency to do so. Such a reaction is, after all, a loss to oneself. Answering is a more important study than asking questions, and they are abandoning the opportunity.

What would Marcus Aurelius do at this case? It's a passage from the Book <Meditations>. (Book5, 20)

"These can impede some activity, yes, but they form no impediments to my impulse or my disposition because here there is conditional commitment and the power of adaptation. The mind adapts and turns round any obstacle to action to serve its objective: a hindrance to a given work is turned to its furtherance, an obstacle in a given path becomes an advance."

Graduation from a master in Financial Engineering

Family photo with Dr. Lane

I graduated from the University of Illinois with a master's degree in Financial Engineering. It is said that a formal diploma will be issued at the end of January. I took a picture of my family with Dr. Lane, a professor of finance and director of our financial engineering program.

And our team practicum, which collaborated with Morgan Stanley, won the 1st prize out of the 11 teams. The grading was conducted through presentations in Chicago, where the scores of judges and the scores of the students attending were combined. Seven members of the team who worked hard took pictures together. All graduates have also been given the title of the financial engineer from now on.

Alpha and Omega in Investment

People usually focus on strategies to find revenue (alpha), but the more important thing is building a reliable trading infrastructure and minimizing fees. And since alpha is soon to disappear after being discovered anyway, it is meaningless to have one great strategy, so always have the right strategies like a pipeline.

A study on life through studying abroad

- I didn't do that, but you'd better finish your necessary education before you're 35, and then live your life using it and adding depth.
- I think my wife and children are by no means my kind of person, but closest friends of life. That is true, and life is comfortable to think so.
- Let's go abroad to study in the U.S. or any other country. Whether young or old, it is challenging to prepare TOEFL or GRE anyway. And life may be hard with studying abroad, but any life is hard. Living without effort doesn't make our lives easier; does it? As Jim Rogers said, Korea is too small to understand and look at the world.

- Koreans are hard-working and good-natured, but the fact that the struggle for survival is excessive is the root of the problem because of the narrowness of land and the concentration of everything in Seoul. Go to many countries around the world and develop your skills and wait for the right time. If South Korea becomes a unified Korea, the Korean Peninsula will be a land of great opportunity.

To sum up, I need to be a beneficial man in the world. No one would refuse or despise me if I were to benefit the world. I got a hint from Marcus Aurelius' <Meditations>. (Book7, 74)

"No one tires of receiving benefit: and action in accordance with nature is your own benefit. Do not then tire of benefit gained by benefit given."

4.2 English: Read English Books Aloud

Read English books aloud

It is essential to read books aloud. Not only English books but also Korean books. That's how it used to be in the past. When you watch historical TV dramas, people read books aloud and rhymes like a song. It may seem funny to modern people, but I realize these days it was the best way to study.

Reading English books aloud is also the best way to train your voice and get healthy while not spending any money. I've purchased mobile apps for English speaking, but they're not fun, and I can't keep doing them. The pattern most of the speaking mobile apps have is that they have a conversation episode organized by subject and situation, and we are supposed to follow it. The problem is that it is annoying to keep up with such living English, and many things have nothing to do with me.

There's no other way. I'm sure there's only one way to study English speaking when you're old. No, this is the best way for all ages. As for me, there is only one way to read aloud the English text of my daily finance book or web page. If you read aloud, not only speaking, but reading and listening are also trained.

One disadvantage is that you can't do it for long because you're physically tired. But, if you keep doing this, you can read an entire book in a matter of hours.

The difference between 'hope' and 'wish'

I have a Financial Engineering project class called practicum this fall semester. I have to choose one of seven companies in Champaign or Chicago as a sponsor, and students are required to write down from first to the third choice.

It takes almost six hours to go back and forth to Chicago, so I hoped for a Champaign practicum because there is no job purpose for me. Most of the other classmates are single and have no family to care for, and most of them want to get a job in Chicago. And they can come back after they have done the project and spent the weekend in Chicago.

At any rate, I had to express my intention briefly, hoping to be sure. However, the Korean translation of 'wish' and 'hope' was similar to each other, but the context was the opposite. 'wish' means wanting something impossible in the form of the subjunctive mood, so in this case, 'hope' is better. "I Hope Champaign practicum. I would appreciate your consideration."

How to train English using iBT TOEFL

Reading

- Read only the first sentence of each paragraph, and the first & last sentence of the last paragraph.

- Read the question first and, if necessary, return to the paragraph and read the required part.
- While you solve various problems, you repeat each paragraph once or twice, so the structure of the entire paragraph is naturally introduced.
- If the words in the text are directly in multiple choices, the chances are high that they are not the answer.
- If you are not sure of the answer, remove the one you are sure it's not the answer, and choose from the rest. (Process of Elimination)

Listening

- Listening well to the first sentence makes sense of purpose of speaking as a whole.
- Listening to understand the other person's purpose and tone of speaking helps him or her to understand the content.
- Remember the content that might come up as a problem in the middle of listening.
- If words from listening are directly in multiple choices, the chances are high that they are not the answer.
- If you are not sure of the answer, remove the one you are sure it's not the answer, and choose from the rest. (Process of Elimination)

Speaking

- Pronunciation and intonation are the most important.
- Memorize the template and keep thinking about what I'm going to say in the content.
- Pause is better than the words "Umm… umm...".
- You should speak clear even one sentence.
- Only if you delivered the points, it would be okay if your words were cut off a little bit at the end.

1) Independent-type speaking (tastes)

```
I think ... ...
First of all, ... ...
For example, ... ...
Also, ... ...
To be specific, ... ...
For these reasons, I think ... ...
```

2) Independent-type speaking (for and against an idea)

```
I agree with the idea that ... ...
First of all, ... ...
For example, ... ...
Also, ... ...
To be specific, ... ...
For these reasons, I totally agree with the idea that ... ...
```

3) Read, listen, and speak (explain others' agree/disagree)

```
The man agrees with the university's decision to ... ...
There are two reasons why he thinks this way.
The first reason is that ... ...
He says that ... ...
The second reason is that ... ...
He says that ... ...
For these reasons, he thinks that the plan is a good idea.
```

4) Read, listen, and speak (explain the professor's examples)

```
According to the reading, ... ...
The professor describes two examples to explain this.
First of all, the professor talks about ... ...
She says that ... ...
Also, the professor talks about ... ...
She says that .... ...
```

5) Listen and speak (identify concerns and present opinions)

```
The woman's problem is that ... ...
The man and the woman discuss two possible solutions.
The first solution is to ... ...
The second solution is to ... ...
I think the second solution is better than the first one.
This is because it will be a waste of time if she ... ...
Also, if she explains her situation to the ... ,
I think the ... will be able to take appropriate action to solve the problem.
For these reasons, I prefer the second solution to the first one.
```

6) Listen and speak (summarize given lecture)

```
In the lecture, the professor describes ... ... by giving some examples.
First of all, the professor talks about ...
He says that ... ...
For example, ... ...
Also, the professor talks about ...
He says that ... ...
For example, ... ...
```

Writing

1) Read, listen, and write

```
In a given statement, the author argues that ... ...
While supporting the argument, however, the author makes numerous assum
ptions which cannot be taken for granted, thus the argument remains unc
onvincing without futher evidence.

Firstly, the author assumes that ... ... ; however this may not be the
case.
... ...
Therefore further evidence pertaining to ... is needed to support the c
laim, as a lack thereof significantly weakens the argument.

Secondly, the argument relies on the assumption that ... ... ; however
there is no sufficient support for this to be convincing.
... ...
Thus, more detailed data are needed to be considered whether ... is ind
eed warranted since the argument is largely based on it.

Lastly, the author assumes that ... .... But it is not plausible that
... ... without corroborating evidence.
... ...
Accordingly, evidence pertaining to ... is necessary to compound the ar
gument.

In conclusion, the author's claim is not very well supported in its cur
rent form. Further evidence pertaining to ..., ... as well as ... is cr
ucial in determining the validity of the claim.
```

2) Independent-type writing

In each paragraph, the topic sentence to claim is preceded by the 'Point' of the PIE structure. And we need examples or research to support this argument, which is 'Illustration' (or Information).

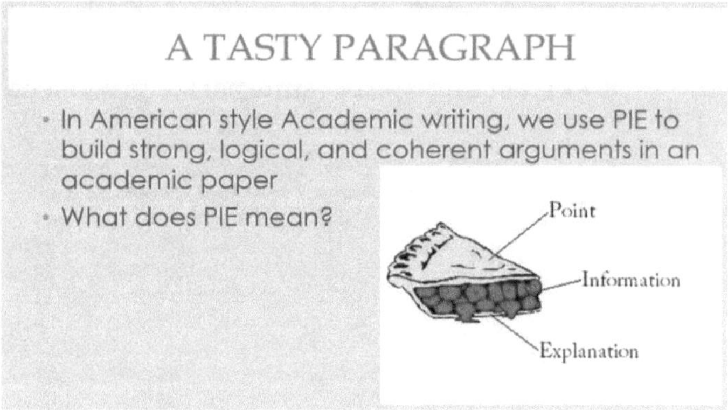

A TASTY PARAGRAPH
In American style Academic writing, we use PIE to build strong, logical, and coherent arguments in an academic paper
What does PIE mean?
Point
Information
Explanation

However, since it is often impossible to know the exact connection between the arguments alone, an 'Explanation' statement must be used to describe this connection.

As it is a paragraph that introduces the whole essay, it needs a 'hook' sentence that can first attract the reader's attention. Then it's better to give a rough 'background' account of the subject and then present 'thesis statement,' which describes what I want to say through the entire article, in one sentence. It is also vital to present the basis of my argument briefly and provide a preview at this time.

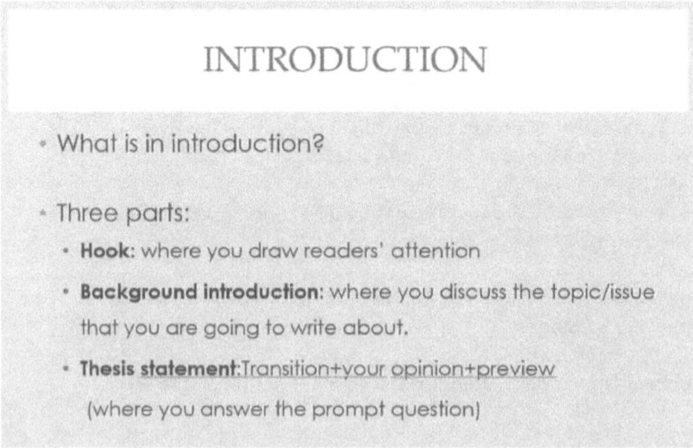

INTRODUCTION
What is in introduction?
Three parts:
Hook: where you draw readers' attention
Background introduction: where you discuss the topic/issue that you are going to write about.
Thesis statement:Transition+your opinion+preview
(where you answer the prompt question)

One caveat is that you should not be humble about what you claim. You should not give the feeling of not knowing well. In other words, expressions like "In my opinion," or "I am not sure about this." is unnecessary.

The conclusion section once again highlights the thesis statement and briefly summarizes the reasons or grounds for which the text has spoken. And you wrap up your thoughts with sentences that call for action or direction of improvement in the future.

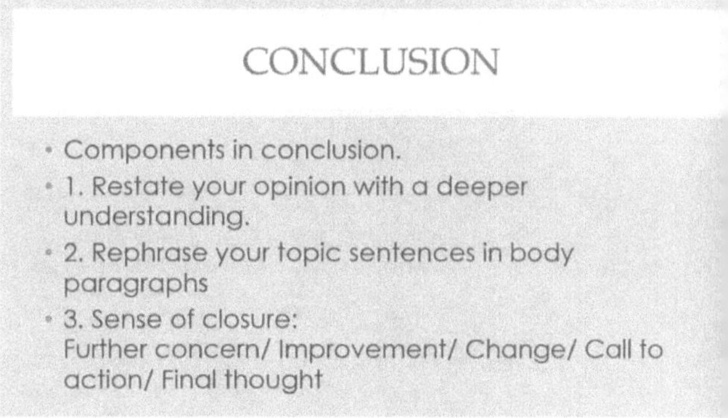

CONCLUSION
• Components in conclusion.
• 1. Restate your opinion with a deeper understanding.
• 2. Rephrase your topic sentences in body paragraphs
• 3. Sense of closure:
Further concern/ Improvement/ Change/ Call to action/ Final thought

These words like "In conclusion," "In summary," "as the essay showed" can be used, but they are unnecessary because they make the thesis weaker. And, of course, the thesis statement is a concept that reinforces the conclusion while it is first presented in the introduction, so it is not appropriate if it comes out first in conclusion. Similarly, new content that is not in the text should not be asserted or explained in conclusion. And it is not good to appeal emotionally in conclusion beyond the nature of the essay.

Still, try

Youngju Nielsen was a successful bond trader on Wall Street after she graduated from college in Korea and studied in the U.S. Currently, she is a professor at Sungkyunkwan University, and I remember reading her book <Seoul to Wall Street> with great interest.

I came to America and was also ignored several times because of my poor English. Instead, it is a bigger problem to lose confidence by not being able to say what I want to say. But

Youngju Nielsen says this experience is also an opportunity to reflect on life more deeply.

Dreams can only be achieved by those who dream, and they can be realized by those who dream vividly. That's the R=VD formula that Lee Ji-sung, a book writer, says. "When you dream vividly, dreams must come true."

외국인·유색인종·여성... '유리천장'은 있다

어디나 그렇듯 월스트리트에도 유리천장이 있다. 인종과 성(性), 국적, 출신지 등이 유리천장을 만든다. 아시아계 황인종, 외국 출신, 그리고 여성인 영주 닐슨에게 월스트리트의 유리천장 이야기를 물었다.

"미국이란 사회가 그렇듯 월스트리트에도 특별한 이유 없이 유색인종을 항상 업신여기고, 미워하는 사람들이 있는 게 사실"이라며 "하지만 미국이란 사회에서 아시아계 유색인종, 여성에게 월스트리트는 그래도 비교적 공정한 곳"이라고 했다.

"최소한 유색인종이기 때문에, 여성이기 때문에 월스트리트 진출에 차별받았다는 말은 과장된 것입니다. 실제론 상당히 많은 수의 유색인종, 여성이 월스트리트에서 활약하고 있습니다. 오히려 유색인종, 외국 출신, 여성의 월스트리트 진출에서 더 큰 걸림돌은 완벽하지 못한 영어와, 2008년 금융위기 이후 더 까다로워진 미국 이민법, 또 미국 출신 백인 남성이 주도하는 매우 정치적인 월스트리트 내부 문화일 겁니다." 그 역시 "그럼에도 유색인종, 외국 출신, 여성에 대한 차별이 아주 없는 것은 아니다"라고 했다.

"많은 수의 유색인종, 외국 출신, 여성이 월스트리트 진출에는 성공하지만, 정작 승진을 하거나 중요한 위치에 발탁되는 이들을 보면 눈에 보이지 않는 월스트리트만의 차별 방식을 알게 됩니다. 고위 임원이나 투자 책임자 같은 자리를 차지한 사람의 절대 다수가 '미국 출신의 백인 남성'입니다. '공정한 평가가 이루어졌다'고 하기에는 월스트리트에서 그렇게 책임 있는 자리에까지 오른 '유색인종, 외국 출신, 여성'의 수가 터무니없이 적다는 게 그 현실을 말해 줍니다. 특히 메이저 투자사에서 이런 경향이 더 심합니다. '미국 출신 백인 남성 vs 유색인종, 외국 출신, 여성'의 구도에서 월스트리트는 분명히 정치적 결정을 내립니다."

영주 닐슨 역시 월스트리트 진출 후 몇몇 백인들 사이에서 소외도 당해봤다. 그의 영어 악센트가 주변의 농담거리가 되는 경험을 하기도 했었다. 하지만 그는 이런 차별이 극복하지 못할 만한 것은 절대 아니라는 점을 강조했다.

영주 닐슨은 오히려 월스트리트는 기회라는 면에서 미국의 다른 그 어떤 영역보다 비교적 공정한 사회라고 했다. 그래서 성(性), 출신지, 인종을 가리지 않고 월스트리트를 꿈꾸는 유능한 젊은이들의 도전이 끊임없이 이어지고 있는 것이라고 했다.

그래도 도전하라

영주 닐슨은 10년이 넘는 월스트리트 생활에서 배운 것이 있다고 했다. '꿈을 꿔야만 꿈을 이룰 수 있다는 것'과 '위험과 불확실성을 감수하지 않고서는 절대 꿈을 이루지 못한다는 것'이 그것이다. 그가 한국의 청년들에게 말했다.

"'한 번도 미국에 가본 적이 없다' 해도 자본시장에서 주인공을 꿈꾸고 있는 청년이라면 망설이지 말고 월스트리트에 도전하세요. 분명히 어눌한 영어 때문에 무시당하는 서러움을 맛볼 겁니다. 인종차별도 당하고, 이방인 취급도 받을 겁니다. 아마도 이제껏 만났던 그 어떤 이들보다 똑똑한 경쟁자들도 숱하게 보게 될 겁니다. 하지만 그 과정에서 더 많은 것을 배울 겁니다. 최소한 무시당하는 서러움을 맛본 만큼 인생과 미래에 대해 더 깊이 있는 고민을 해볼 수 있게 될 겁이다. 그것이 세계 최고의 무대 월스트리트에 한 발짝 더 다가서게 하는 힘이 돼줄 것입니다. 후회를 할지언정 해보고 후회하는 게 더 나으니까요."

A magazine article about Youngju Nielsen's lesson

4.3 Life: Don't Ask a Human

Used electronic keyboard

I bought a used electronic keyboard for $60, and my wife is delighted. She initially liked playing the piano in Korea, and it seems to be very helpful to relieve the stress of her. One problem is that she wants to take it to Korea when we return, but probably it will cost more than $60 for transportation. It exceeds the plane's baggage specification.

Casio electronic keyboard

Mobile electronic wallet, Google Pay

Last time I bought a lot of things at the mart and tried to pay, I found that I didn't bring my wallet. I would have come home empty-handed if we hadn't gone with Zhanna, next door neighbor (photo below). Since then, I have installed Google Pay on my smartphone for the first time. When I put it on the card terminal today, it worked well with a tingling sound.

Samsung Pay, which also works on magnetic terminals, was popular in Korea, where the penetration rate of NFC terminals is low, but Samsung Pay is unlikely to be needed in the U.S. Since most stores, including mart, have legal restrictions on using magnetic terminals for security reasons, mostly NFC terminals have been installed, so the iPhone's Apple Pay or the Android phone's Google Pay is enough. And it doesn't seem like much time left for Samsung Pay in Korea, either. That is because most of the current magnetic cards are being changed to IC chips.

ALDI mart payment terminal

Also, Samsung Pay is only available on the latest Galaxy Note 5 or higher smartphones with LoopPay technology, but Google Pay, on the other hand, is available on any Android phone with NFC functionality. For your information, these mobile electronic wallets are available online as well as offline.

Rowing machine exercise

- The lower body must lead the rowing. You have to take your hips out first, and your upper body should follow.
- Keep your shoulders straight without recoil. Avoid pushing your shoulders out when releasing.
- Don't lean back too much. Your upper body is right for 11 o'clock when pulled and 1 o'clock when released.

Concept2 rowing machine in the school gym

Principle of social life

The tenets of company life I think are as follows. That is the same as social life in that the expansion of company life is social life.

It is the desire of all human beings to be recognized and promoted well in the company and to rise to a higher position. For this to be realized, the higher my influence on the company, the more likely it is. And to be an influential person, the better the skill, the more likely it is.

The better my skills, the more self-directed I can work, but the more important thing is to have a good relationship with my boss because it is a structure in which my boss determines my destiny. Also, people often have to be helped by others to get their achievements in the company, which affects their performance. Anyway, it is the essence of the company life that there is no end to internal politics and the fight for own interest. But it is minor in the long run, so the greed of the moment should not sway me.

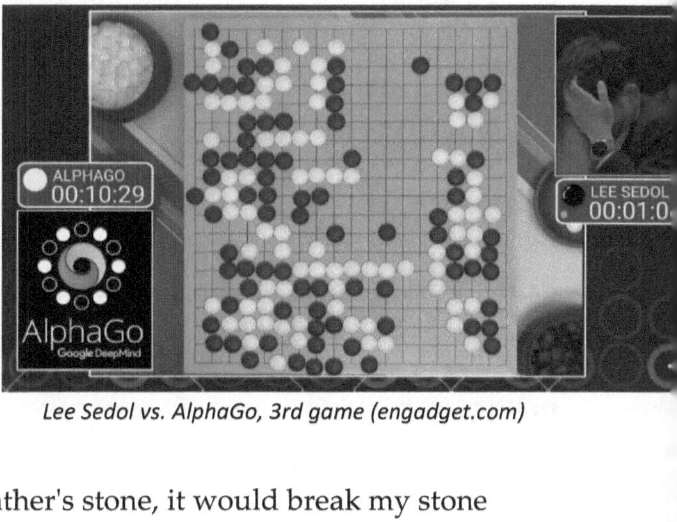

Lee Sedol vs. AlphaGo, 3rd game (engadget.com)

It's better to have the feeling of connecting me with people. When I played Baduk with my father when I was young, I always heard that if I connect all my stones, it will never die. If I tried to force myself to catch my father's stone, it would break my stone before long, and it would soon be in jeopardy. If I think about it now, this connection seems closest to the reality of social influence. There is an official networking time for academic conferences and gatherings in the United States, not to be viewed negatively.

One thing is that one's ability that is meaningful only in that company is of no great use. It's worth risking my life to do something that can be used elsewhere. It's remarkable what I've done and what skills I have, and it's not essential what company I've worked for. That's how the world is changing, and that's a right direction.

The attitude we should have about our work life should be the same as that of Marcus Aurelius, the king of Rome, treated court affairs in the <Meditations>. (Book6, 12)

"If you had a step-mother and a mother at the same time, you would pay attention to your step-mother but nevertheless your constant recourse would be to your mother. That is now how it is with the Court and philosophy. So return to philosophy again and again, and take your comfort in her: she will make the other life seem bearable to you, and you bearable in it."

Google Chrome Shortcuts

Since the Chrome browser was born in 2008, it has already been more than ten years. It broke the stronghold of Internet Explorer and now holds the largest market share of 60 percent. IE or Firefox is about 12%. The Chrome browser is becoming a platform that can be used in the same environment anywhere in Windows, MacOS, Android, and beyond. Something rather heavy is a blemish.

My favorite shortcut is to return to the previous page by pressing Alt+Left Arrow. And when the screen is narrow, I often watch it in full-screen mode with F11. Zooming in and out with Ctrl+Plus or Minus key is also sometimes useful.

When bookmarks increase and need to be managed, they can be accessed directly by Ctrl+Shirt+O. Ctrl+Tab is handy for switching between open tabs, and it is also very convenient to scroll through the screen using a space bar. And if the cached image is not updated immediately and a cache deletion is required, the menu is accessible directly with the Ctrl+Shift+Del.

Carle Hospital emergency

I took Jamilia, the daughter of Zhanna next door, to Carl Hospital emergency in the morning for vomiting and headache. She said that the left eye was sick and dizzy. It seems that she has had one or two such symptoms before. I'm glad to hear that Jamilia's social security insurance covers it.

Carle Hospital Emergency

Don't ask a human

Miserable and stuffy while doing homework over the weekend, other thoughts came to mind. It was an e-book that I stumbled upon while searching on Google, and it was fascinating. The author seems to have gained enlightenment through reading books, as he deals with some philosophical content, such as what life is, why people are living, and what relationship God and the universe have. First of all, it was very realistic to explain his childhood life and family history clearly, and overall, I felt the depth of his worries, and I sympathized with him. I soon fell in love with this e-book. The story of 12 years of studying in Germany was also impressive.

I bought this book for about $4 at the Google Bookstore since I had a $10 Google gift card that I had just received. It is not available in a paper book. The author, who uses the name 'brother' said he had asked countless people about life, religion, the universe, and the problems of death, but did not get a satisfactory answer, and that he happened to meet with 'Him' and finally realized that 'He' had come to him. In other words, a person who is destined to die cannot know the agony of death. The title <Don't Ask a Human> means that.

Many people live happily without worrying about what life is and what happiness is. He concludes that **everything is meaningful as it is, so you just have to watch and live your life faithfully**. The author majored in architecture in Germany and is currently a professor of architectural engineering at Kwangwoon University and seems to be about 60 years old. After watching the movie 'The Matrix' and reading the novel 'Snow Crash,' he fell in love with virtual reality and spent 20 years building a virtual city but failed twice and is said to be trying again. He believes the information revolution that Peter Drucker talked about would be the virtual reality.

Clark-Lindsey silver town in Urbana

We went to the Clark-Lindsey silver town near my house to celebrate its 40th anniversary. The atmosphere was good because there were good food and musical performance.

One of my bucket lists is a Europe busking trip with my family, and in that sense, today's performance was awe-inspiring. Even though it was a one-person performance, the recording function of the amplifier was used to make chords for the performer himself, creating a rich effect as if several sessions were playing together. It seems to be a beneficial device for busking.

Lunch and guitar performance

Small miniature horses came as guests to help relieve stress on the elderly. Taeju was busy touching, and Taye ran away, saying that the dog looked strange.

Miniature horses for the mental health of elderly

About fairness

When I think back, I was mostly angry when I felt unfair. I've had it a few times in my career. There was a head worker of my team who said that the world isn't fair anyway. I said I thought the world was almost fair, but then he suggested to make a bet. I was glad I didn't bet then. Now, I think he's right.

An entirely equitable world is similar to what finance calls a complete market. An ideal market in which all information is reflected in the price and no transaction costs at all. The essence of trading is to balance an unbalanced market, so without transaction costs, the market would be much easier to find balance.

The beauty of the human world, of the financial market, is that it is no less complete than that it is not so incomplete. There is difficulty in our response that it is not perfect but relatively close to complete.

In other words, the dichotomous idea of complete and incomplete makes a proper response difficult. There are many good people in the world, but there are also many bad guys. But they all only occupy a position of a normal distribution, and there is no absolute good or absolute evil in the world.

Unemployment is the future

I happened to watch EBS talk by Dr. Ko Mi-Sook, whom I admire, on YouTube. The theme is 'Unemployment is the future.' Her book, <Homo Kungfus>, is a book that has had a significant impact on my life. Dr. Ko says she first created the career of a classical critic. Before that, it was up to the scholars to interpret the classics, and her work was the first practical interpretation of classics aimed at applying life from the beginning.

I'm not afraid to be unemployed, either. But wouldn't it be necessary for humans to do what I want to do and also to make at least enough money to make a living out of it? I want to enjoy the real freedom in which this is satisfied.

Dr. Ko Mi-Sook on EBS program

Facial exercises

Facial expression plays a critical role in interpersonal relationships. That is because facial expressions reveal a person's feelings. So blunt or negative impressions may cause unnecessary misunderstandings. There is nothing like a mirror to check your posture or expression and practice.

It's not good to try to hide your feelings in order to hide negative facial expressions. Not only is it not working, but it is not desirable to separate one's body from one's emotions. Instead, try to control your emotions. When you manage emotions, negative emotions are reduced, and facial expressions are revived.

A person's emotions are like driving a bicycle, which is something that must be controlled so that it doesn't deviate much from the center.

Sponsored training vs. Leave of absence

Even now, with only a few days left to graduate, one of the questions I am often asked is whether I got sponsorship from my company. In other words, people are asking me if my company sent me as sponsored training because they think I came here to study at a little old age. It's hard to explain, so I only gloss over it, but I don't feel happy to answer because I have awkward circumstances to tell.

I was going to study abroad for my company's overseas education training, and I was going to receive financial support such as tuition and living expenses. However, the admission that I received is more than four months over one year of the education period that was originally announced. Eventually, I was forced to take a leave of absence at my own expense, instead of sponsored education. I suffered a lot from financial damage as well as from my relationship with the company and, above all, felt my lack of influence.

My company believed that there was no formal prior consultation. But I think this is an overly passive attitude in the circumstances. It was discussed verbally with the head of the human resources team in advance that my goal is to conduct a financial engineering course that has been somewhat over a year. And I received an e-mail stating that they would provide guidelines for support after a review if I submitted my programs that were scheduled to be applied, and that I responded by specifying the current financial engineering course at the University of Illinois as 15 months.

And, even if I concede, it would be reasonable to treat the one year at the company's expense and the other four months at my own cost. It was in April 2017, and I was advised to apply again for the reason that some schools still have time to apply.

But, it felt to me that it was not an alternative but an administrative expedient.

After struggling with my company for more than a month, I realized that it was impossible for an employee to fight against one's company alone in terms of balance of power, and that I applied for a leave of absence at my own expense because it was more important for me to go abroad to study than money.

It's been a long time, and it's probably because of my lack of ability. If I study abroad hard and make more money later, I think this regret will be healed.

Planet Fitness

I didn't know that the U.S. fitness center was this cheap and good. Ten dollars a month. Of course, the annual fee is 39 dollars a year, and taxes are extra, but it's still less expensive. The facilities are excellent, and the staff is even kind. I enjoy working out at Planet Fitness every morning. As their copy says, it's not a Gym; it's another Planet.

Replace laptop keyboard myself

A few days ago, seven keys were mangled in a laptop. The keys gathered nearby did not work, including the keys 8, 9, and 0. Unfortunately, it happened a day after Taye spat on the keyboard while watching the movie. I don't think it's going to be such a problem, but I don't know the exact reason why. No matter how hard I find a way to deal with it, I have to repair it at my own expense after a year in the warranty period. Eighty-five dollars for diagnosis alone, and 150 dollars for parts alone, which would probably cost 300 dollars.

This 2-in-1 laptop was more difficult as only the keyboard was not come out separately, and the entire c-cover was made into a single piece to make it thinner. In other words, the keyboard unit and the bottom panel of the laptop were put together with thinly, and if even one key failed, the entire lower board had to be replaced.

Finally, I decided to buy a used lower board (c-cover) for $69 on eBay and replace it myself. The seller looked like a person who sold parts professionally, and it was like a new one as it was a refurbished product. Lenovo Yoga 710 Hardware Maintenance Manual, which was found on the Internet by my wife, was also a great help.

To replace the entire board, the main board, the cooling fan, SSD, speakers, fingerprint reader, and various connectors had to be removed first. Eventually, after two and a half hours of work and testing, the laptop became newer and more robust than it was before, and after a few disassembly and assembly, it became understandable inside my computer.

Ready to replace keyboard

My laptop is Yoga 710-15IKB, and there were mostly 710-15ISK parts on eBay. But IKB meant CPU platform Kaby Lake and ISK implied Skylake, so I expected the bottom plate to be the same structure and finally hit it. And the base cover was fastened with ten screws, and it was a star-shaped hexagon screw, so it needed a T5 Torx screwdriver. It's like a screw for MacBook Air, while all the internal boards are fastened with Phillips screws.

Honda CR-V power steering motor

I was going to come home after morning exercise, but the handle wouldn't move. A handle-shape light on the instrument panel called MIL (Malfunction Indicator Light) was illuminated to indicate the failure. Since the power steering is not working, it is harder to move the handle in a standstill than to lift a 60-pound barbell. The drop-in temperature below minus 25 degrees Celsius seems to have affected it. I managed to drive home carefully, but it's hard to get around like this.

Power steering used to be operated by a hydraulic pump, but these days, it is powered by electric power steering (EPS). So, it doesn't use any hydraulic oil at all, so no concerns about leakage, but I checked and found that the price of the parts is significant. eBay was selling EPS motor racks from the car it crashed into for around $150, but it was very embarrassing to see the picture of the crashed car.

I checked again in the afternoon when the weather was a little warmer, and fortunately, it returned to normal. It is said to be the first cold snap in 30 years, and it is speculated that the moisture inside the motor has frozen. Anyway, I checked the Diagnostic Trouble Code with my $15, OBD2 vehicle scanner, and it came out OK. It was fortunate that life was so inconvenient without a car in the U.S. and it cost a lot of money to fix it.

Find my phone

I lost my cell phone in the arboretum near my house. The pants I bought last time have such shallow pockets that things keep getting out of it. I didn't know at all because it was a field with grass, so I couldn't hear a sound of phone drop. Unfortunately, it suddenly snowed and was covered with white snow, and three or four rounds of the search were made but could not be found.

After a few hours, I thought about searching for Android phones, so I tried typing 'find my phone' on Google. There was a five-minute service that made sounds on my device. It said it would make a sound regardless of whether my phone was in vibrating mode or not. If my phone weren't in vibration mode, I would have already called someone else's phone to track the sound. At any rate, my phone was ringing in the snow when I searched for a possible neighborhood with this method. Ah...I saw it. It feels like founding wild ginseng in the snow.

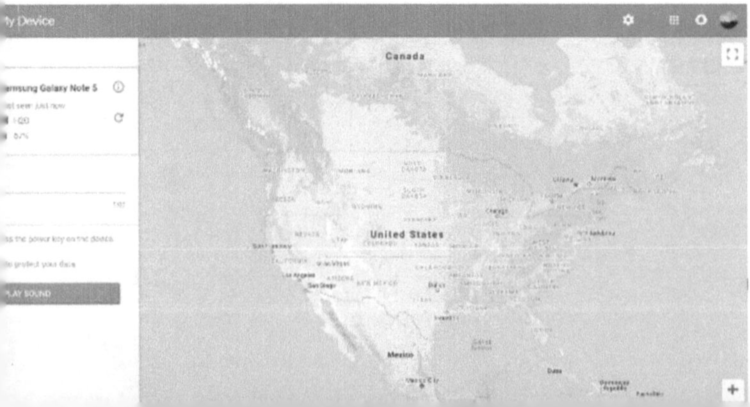

ester (Fall 2018)

4.4 Parenting: Infantile Dependency Needs

My second Quad Day

The University of Illinois holds a club promotion event, Quad Day, just before the end of the summer break and the beginning of the fall semester. So, this day naturally marked the beginning of the new school year.

I remember that it was scorching on Quad Day in 2017, as well as in this year. What is interesting is that August had been refreshing and cold even a few days ago, but the weather has been hot all of a sudden since yesterday. Indeed, the weather in Illinois is very variable. As for financial options, it would be better to have high volatility, but the weather is more desirable to have low volatility.

There was a piano in the Illini Union cafe, and a man was playing. My children danced and played frantically on the platform to the song. On the other side, there is a Starbucks, and many Koreans are sitting there. I saw more Koreans than Chinese in school today.

Inside the Illini Union

Maybe it's a swimming club, putting tubes on swimsuits and promoting them, while the martial arts club is busy doing somersaults on the lawn.

There was also a man in Hanbok, Korean traditional clothing, who looked a little hot because of the weather.

Camping chairs that I bought in Meijer on the last Independence Day played a proper role today. I took my kids to Quad Day with two camping chairs in a bike trailer, and I sat under a tree and rested. Compared to last year, it's heaven. My children and wife went around a booth to find something like candy. As I sat in the middle of the lawn, I could meet two classmates to greet them.

My kids resting at the camping chair

Taye did not try to move at all at the train booth. Taye's love of trains, cars, is great. We took a look around for ten minutes there, but he didn't try to go while crying.

Instinctive jealousy

Looking into the heart of a child is like looking inside an adult. A few days ago, my wife kept saying that Taye was so cute, so Taeju suddenly called her mom for the reason that she had taken a pee on the floor of the toilet. Taeju is past the age of making such a mistake in the bathroom. Taeju seems to have lied to her mom. From the standpoint of Taeju, she doesn't want her mom to like her younger brother more than her, and I think Taeju even disliked Taye.

At this situation, it is essential for parents to understand and empathize with their child's mind. Jealousy is a natural, by no means strange, one of the many emotions a human can have. However, if a child's jealousy is too much, parents need to intervene and control it at the right time. And, you'd better let her know, "As an older sister, you may very hard because you have to give in to your brother, but you have a better side. There are other things you can do with your parents even though your brother can't."

It is human nature to envy others for being praised and doing well. However, it would be even more unbearable if it was not because of his efforts but because of his tricks. And this is when you want someone in power to step in and correct it.

The same is true of organizational life. There are bound to be second-in-command in addition to first-in-command in any organization. Everyone can't help the No. 1 man because the organization has empowered him. But the No. 2 person can be anyone, and it's common to be the person whom No. 1 person likes mostly. There are a lot of messy emotional fights to get this job. And the responsibility lies in fact with the No. 1 man. A good leader should not be a king himself using the No. 2 man, but a man of empathy who can look at people who belong to the organization.

Taeju pushing cart in the mart

Happy to play a role

Children around the age of Taeju appear to be eager to do what they can. Pushing the cart at the mart is one of them. She's still clumsy, so I'm afraid of hitting someone else, but if she wants to, I'm willing to leave it to her. I think she feels the sense of accomplishment that she is needed in this family and will feel a sense of existence as an older sister that she can do it even though her younger brother can't.

Taye's toilet training

Taye turned three years old, and it's time to take off his diaper through toilet training. I'm frustrated with his slow progress, but we don't rush him because he'll undoubtedly take off his diaper one day.

Because the toilet was so big and high that Taye couldn't climb up, I bought a hard container and made a simple urinal. Usually, he urinates there during the day, but on some days, he is not consistent, asking mom to wear a diaper. If he doesn't wear diapers, his mom's touch is less likely to reach him, so I think Taye's diapers are a bit strategic.

Infantile dependency needs

Adult personality and identity are mostly formed by experience when young. So, if you look closely at the growing process of children and the mind, you will realize the human nature itself.

The most popular keyword in the book <Why am I conscious of others> is 'infantile dependency needs.' The main point of the book is that all of the problems of human nature are due to the incomplete fulfillment of infantile dependency needs as a child. And the bigger problem than not being met is that one's infantile dependency needs, which one has failed to acknowledge and be filled by one's pride as an adult, are unwittingly manifested in the other side of bullying, excessive devotion and excess showing-off.

During reading this book, I felt like I solved a puzzle. There are many good people in the world, but there are far more people who don't, and there is no enough cognitive theory to explain it. Instead, it makes more sense to tell that many adults in the world are not fully grown up because they were not cared for properly as infants, and when they become adults, they hide it and live it. Anyone can only grow psychologically by accepting this fact.

Some people try to fill this deficiency by dating, and some people ask their wives and children, and even their subordinates. Of course, as people grow up, they can't admit that they want to be childish like a child, so hide it unconsciously. But still, the unfulfilled desire to rely on others makes them more distrustful and aggressive.

Some grew up in a harmonious family with warm care, but others may not. However, infantile dependency needs are never fulfilled in social life based on the Give-and-Take of adults. It is said that infantile dependence needs are only filled when I take it for granted and when I realize that I am worthy of it. That's why we need someone who can share our minds.

Krannert Center Family Day

The Krannert Center is like a concert hall at the University of Illinois. Built in 1969, it was holding various 50th-anniversary events from this year to next year. This Saturday morning it had Family Day, so I took the children there despite the rainy weather. While we, parents would like to see Yo-Yo Ma's cello or Lang Lang's piano performances more, children would be happier playing in the lobby like this.

Krannert Center Family Day

Lunch at King School

Ah'Miracle is a black kid who lives near the school and has a kind personality, so she kept talking to us and trying to help. Taye was so cute that she showed the kindness of giving his apple sauce to Taye. Elyona is a black child from France, considering she can speak French and will look very pretty when she grew up. Nouran is a child from Egypt, and I think I've seen her at a community center. Eliot is a playful white boy, and he was very fond of Taye, saying that Taye looks like a pug.

Taeju's chips overeating

There was a Movie Night at the Orchard Downs Community Center last night, so my wife took two children there. I heard that Taeju ate too many chips while watching the movie. Taeju did not eat food well, so I didn't usually buy snacks. Anyway, Taeju ate three bags of chips by herself that day.

While she fell asleep, she suddenly said she had a stomachache, and Taeju threw up all over the bedclothes. After throwing up twice like this, I thought it would be okay in the morning, so I sent her to school. At lunch, my wife got a call from King School that Taeju got her lunch and soon threw up, so come and take her.

I drove to the school office, and Taeju was sleeping in an office chair with her backpack in her hand. Her face looked pale and so bad, and I was wondering if there was not any medical room in this school. If it were in Korea, I would have asked the staff why they laid her down on the office chair. It's hard to explain the situation in English, so I just took her with me.

Later on, on second thought, the school put her on standby in an office chair to send her home, but she just fell asleep in a chair. Anyway, I brought her home to rest, and she recovered a lot after eating pumpkin porridge and bananas that her mom made in the evening. The next day was Friday, so I just let her rest for another day.

Toilet paper corner is a heaven for kids

Get rid of baby teeth and get fresh teeth

Everyone except Taeju is said to have new teeth in the school class. The Western and Indian races certainly seem to be growing fast. My wife is worried about why Taeju's permanent teeth aren't coming out, but in fact, I think Taeju's teeth are cuter now.

Dad and daughter selfie

Child constipation

I was worried about Taeju's stool because it was so hard that it couldn't come out. I was even more shocked when my wife asked me if she should dig it out with fingers. In case of emergency, I thought we should take her to the emergency room, but it's not easy to take her to the hospital because it's so cold these days. Next day, I searched the internet quickly and bought a sedentary type of 'Preparation H' and waited.

The next day, after drinking a lot of milk, my wife said that Taeju took her poop well. Oh no. Should I only keep it as a household medicine?

Taking photos of Taeju's class

Taeju took a necklace from home to take a picture. What kind of looks does she care so much about? She doesn't resemble her mom or dad's fashion sense at all.

Class photo of Mrs. Spencer-Tanner class

Composition of Taeju

American schools consider that writing education is essential. Last time, as I heard in the parent-teacher conference day, Taeju's writing skills were not as excellent as those of the first grade, but she has improved a lot these days and has come closer.

> "I want to be a unicorn because I can use my horn to make a magic. I will use my magic to fly into the sky, and I will use my magic to go down again. And the next day, I will use my magic to touch the cloud, and I will go to sleep. (The end)"

All the songs are rap

Interestingly enough, all the songs Taeju learns are like rap, as there are many black children at Martin Luther King, Jr. Elementary School. And even though she knows Obama, she has no idea who Trump is.

One day on Taeju's birthday, we bought a cupcake in the classroom and gave it to children to eat, when they suddenly sang 'Happy Birthday Taeju' like a rap. It's the feeling to be seen only in movies, such as 'Oh Happy Day.'

These days, there is a rap that Taeju sings and memorizes frequently.

> "When you look up at the night sky, what do you see? The moon glows above. That's me. I don't make my own light like a sun or a star. I reflect the sunlight through the night is all."

Taye's preschool re-trial

Urbana Early Childhood School is a local public preschool. Taye is now past the age of three to enter a preschool. There is an Orchard Downs preschool in front of our house, but it is impossible unless the child is toilet-trained.

When, last time, Taye was screened for admission to a public preschool here, he failed because he refused to take the test. When the teacher asked him questions, he had to answer in Korean or English, but he did not respond at all by holding on his mom. From Kinder, everyone has to go to compulsory education, but a preschool is an option, so they test whether a child's development is at a certain level and get only the right children.

On the way to Urbana Early Childhood School

After many twists and turns, I managed to get a chance to re-screens a month and a half later, and fortunately, he answered much better this time. On the way in, school buses resting in groups made him feel better. Usually, 80 percent of Taye's head is packed with school buses and the rest with fire trucks. And I motivated him to go to McDonald's for lunch if he answers well, so he worked hard. There's a PlayPlace inside McDonald's, so he can slide around and have fun. The screening results will be notified later after the final review by the principal.

McDonald PlayPlace

4.5 Culture: Remember Through Donation

Remember through donation

Entering the children's library from the Urbana Library, there is Megan's reading room on one side. It is a space where parents and children can read books or play with ease. On the sign in front of the room, it was donated by the family to commemorate Megan Spitze (1985-1988). I don't know what the reason is, but they gave this space to remember their granddaughter, who passed away at only three years old. I searched the Internet to find out why, but I couldn't find it, but only the local newspaper reported that Megan's grandmother, Hazel Spitze, died in 2009 at the age of 86.

It's too bad that the child has left the world at an early age, but I think if there is another way to remember it in a better and more harmonious way. Thanks to this Megan's reading room, even people from faraway countries like me are already connected to this child who is not in the world. The connection through Facebook or Instagram is far less graceful than this.

Megan's reading room in Urbana Library

Economically, it's like a zero-sum game because the Spitze family paid for and residents have free access to the facility, but in fact, it's a plus-sum game where both get what they want. Regardless of profit and loss, what economist Alfred Marshall called a 'warm heart' would be more like this.

Roots of Western culture

Looking at Wall Street's hedge fund names, Greek gods often appear. If you put 'capital' behind the god names Zeus, Ares, Hermes, Poseidon, and Athena, you'll see that dizzying hedge funds are all searched. Of course, the Roman names of the same god are Jupiter, Mars, Mercury, Neptune, and Minerva. There are even 'Hades Capital' after the terrible god of death.

Solar planets and their satellites were all borrowed from Greek and Roman mythology. Even the names of the spaceships are the same, so the first spacecraft to land on the moon is Apollo 11.

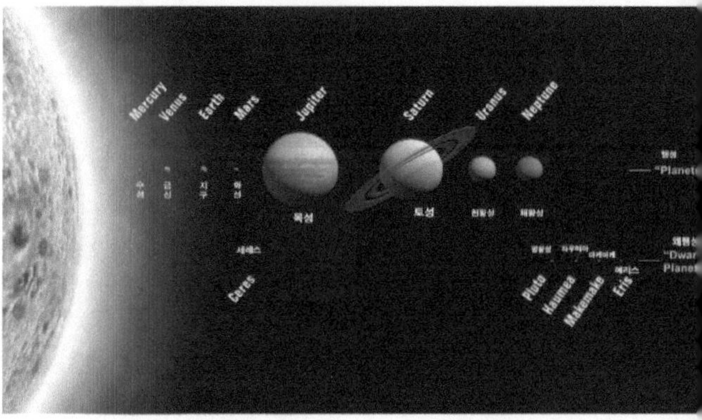

The name of the solar system

Kim Hun, a professor at Seoul National University, is an expert in Western classics who has long lectured on Greek and Roman mythology. He said the loneliness of our lives might be due to the lack of lifetime classics. Since Greek and Roman mythology, the Bible, or the Analects of Confucius are all good, I will have to be with a classic for the rest of my life.

Groupism vs. Individualism and Balance

In Korea, there is still a culture of groups, so people try to subjugate those who are inferior to themselves, and they try to submit to those who are better than themselves to ensure their survival. If they think about it, they are doing it unconsciously and culturally. It's a little bit closer to the world of animals where everything is sequenced.

On the other hand, most Americans say they can't tolerate others harming them. So, in the world of most adults, they don't like to rank, and they only need to let others not disturb their survival in horizontal relationships. Donation culture can also be seen as favoring one's survival in the long run.

If the land is small and the population is dense, it will naturally be easy for others to interfere with my survival. Despite trying to control effectively through laws and systems, the only fundamental way is to maintain a proper distance between people. That is the state of balance that science and engineering say. The sun is indispensable to humans, but it is precious because it continues to maintain a proper distance, or equilibrium, from the Earth.

Martin Luther King, Jr. Day

Every year in the United States, the third Monday of January is celebrated as Martin Luther King, Jr. Day. Martin Luther King, Jr. is a considerable spiritual force among black Americans. As you can see from the life of a black jazz diva, Billie Holiday, it is inevitable to think of the discrimination and hardship of blacks in the 1960s and 1970s. Perhaps up until the 1980s, the history of the ordeal continued.

There is some inevitability about ability discrimination in a capitalist society.

Martin Luther King Jr. Day ceremony

However, just ignoring people by the difference in the color of the skin is excessive racism of some white people.

Cannabis (Marijuana)

Orchard Downs study room sometimes has a strong smell of burning grass. Maybe the person who lives in the other house is smoking marijuana in the bathroom. When I googled it, I found that it smells like burning grass, which is quite similar. I'd instead do it outside. Why smoke in the bathroom and smell the whole building?

I come here study room sometimes, but I think people living in this building are going to be a lot more painful. In the U.S., many feel it is useless to report the case to the police unless it is the current criminal. For now, it's my job only to keep the bathroom door shut and turn the ventilator around.

Currently, marijuana for medical purposes is legal in thirty U.S. states, while marijuana for recreational purposes is legal in Washington, D.C., and nine states. Illinois is a state for which medical purposes are legitimate but recreational purposes are not. And in the U.S., marijuana is called cannabis. Anyway, there seems to be a considerable difference between the perception of marijuana in Korea and that of Americans. Obama also said in his autobiography that he had smoked marijuana.

Philosophy of simplicity, minimalism

I thought the pioneer of minimalism was Japanese, but the U.S. is even a step ahead. Japan has been making up a lot of things, and now they try to get back to basics, but the U.S. has not even tried to make it up at all.

The signboards seem to stick letters to standard forms. The shape of the house is simple. The desk and furniture were cut from wood, but there is no sign of beauty. Water fountain, toilet sink, and toilet are almost the same shapes and same brand. It's like a communist country. Cars can hardly find electric mirrors or electronic air conditioners other than just the right equipment.

Anyway, for minimalism to be possible at home, there must be many storage spaces and a cover on them. That's the way our house is structured, but it is so full of things due to the children. I don't think we can practice minimalism until ten years after the children grow up and become independent.

Simple and uniform signboard of the U.S.

Cornhole, a traditional American game

I played the classic American game called Cornhole at the Savoy Church. There is a hole in the board, and the board has a slope. Put it on both sides and play each other's turn, betting on who puts a lot of pockets in the hole or on the board. In the church, we played 2:2, and had one point on the board and three points in the hole. If you score 15 points first, the game will end.

Traditional North American game, Cornhole (wikipedia)

I tried it with Clint several times and got good results in its way. One trick is to throw your pocket higher than 45 degrees. If you throw it low to put it right in the hole, it won't go in, but because of the inertia towards the front, your pocket keeps moving out of the plate. The wooden board is painted and slippery. On the other hand, if you throw it into a parabola, the pocket will be more likely to climb onto the board even if it doesn't get into the hole. Of course, it's a story when your posture is somewhat stable.

Closing

Finally, I want to finish this book by referring to my thought of happiness. Everything I do, including studying in the U.S. at the age of 44, is for me to be happy in the end. As Monk Hyemin said, altruistic acts for others are all acts for me if you go deep into them.

According to my 20 years of research solely on intuition, human happiness is a relative concept. The absolute happiness that man feels never lasts long. Even if you're $10 million rich, you'll soon find dissatisfaction with something else. Praying to God does not change the nature of man. And asking for a change in nature is not appropriate as a request to the God who created us. Rather, humans feel much greater happiness in comparison with others or with me of yesterday. However, since there is no end to comparisons with others, my life will eventually become miserable. So, my conclusion is that in order for humans to feel happy, they must create happiness through themselves better than yesterday's.

It's best to feel happy through yourself developing every day. But when that is not possible, one way is to make me a little bit suffer today enough to handle. I once slept in a tent for 10 days during an outdoor training session in the middle of winter in the army and returned to my quarters. It was a very cold room without heating, but it was much more comfortable than the tent, and I realized this was real happiness. If you want to be happy, set up a tent in the backyard and sleep tonight. Being able to sleep at home tomorrow will be happiness in itself.

(End)

Author: Jongnam Kim (김종남, 金鍾男)

He likes to read, think, and sweat.

His motto is to study and give it to others.

His dream is to be a man of world benefit.

He studied mathematics education, computer engineering at Seoul National University, and financial engineering at the University of Illinois.

(*jongnam.kim@gmail.com*)

This book was self-published, so I need to promote this book myself. If you have enjoyed reading, please review or comment briefly on Amazon.com. It will be a great help to me.

Thank you for reading!

Jongnam

www.ingramcontent.com/pod-product-compliance
Lightning Source LLC
Chambersburg PA
CBHW061337280526
45784CB00001B/43
9781097371839